ARCHERY

BODY AND MIND

The Complete Mental and
Physical Training System for Archers

JONATHAN CLEMINS

JONATHAN CLEMINS

Printed Worldwide
First Printing 2025
First Edition 2025

10 9 8 7 6 5 4 3 2 1

Interior Book Design by Walt's Book Design
www.waltsbookdesign.com

ARCHERY

Body and Mind

"No man has the right to be an amateur in the matters of physical training. It is a shame for a man to grow old without seeing the beauty and strength of which the body is capable."

-SOCRATES

ABOVE ALL ELSE

To the archers who put their trust in me, not just as a coach, but as a friend in pursuit of something meaningful. You've given me purpose, passion, and the chance to grow alongside you.

Thank You.

TABLE OF CONTENTS

INTRODUCTION

The Mirror Shift

I was coaching a high school archer a number of years ago, and one day after practice, he asked about working out and asked for my help. We discussed the basics like bodyweight exercises, light lifting, and core stability. I gave him some suggestions, a simple plan to follow, and we scheduled a time to meet for a workout together.

One week after starting to work out, he started a fitness profile on Instagram. While part of me found it amusing, the other part was incredibly interested. In what universe does this make sense? His body hadn't changed, not in one week, but his energy had. He stood taller. He behaved with more confidence. There was a spark that wasn't there before.

And that's when it hit me: the mirror hadn't changed, but the way he looked into it had. It was in this moment that I realized there had to be something more going on than just physical changes, but mental changes, too. That's the real power of training. Yes, fitness matters, a stronger body and more endurance, but the first gains often appear in the mind. Confidence grows, mood improves, and you start to believe in yourself. And that mental shift translates straight into performance on the line, in the classroom, and in life.

That's what many archers overlook. Exercise isn't just about how you look. It's a transformative mental shift.

Why This Book? Why Now?

Everybody knows that exercise makes us feel better, but do you know why? The reason we feel so good when we exercise is that it helps our brain function at its best. The point of exercise for archery is to build and condition the brain. With this book, my hope is that if you understand how exercise enhances mental performance, you'll be motivated to incorporate it into your training.

In the last few decades, sports science has made something abundantly clear: the mental game is not a bonus; it's the foundation. For elite performers, whether Olympic athletes, concert violinists, or military sharpshooters, the difference between good and great lies between the ears.

Archery is a sport of control. It demands focus without overthinking. But you can't simply "decide" to be calm or confident at full draw when your heart is racing, and the wind picks up. Those conditions must be trained, rehearsed, and strengthened like any other muscle.

Yet so many archers treat mental training as something to work on only when something goes wrong. I see and hear so many social media posts that say, "I need to work on my mental game." Archers understand the importance of the mental game, but many aren't sure HOW to work on improving their mental performance. This book flips that script.

The Two Pillars of Performance

The book is divided into two parts, each addressing a core pillar of high performance:

Part 1: Train the Body, Shape the Mind

The body doesn't just perform the shot; it shapes the mind that executes it. When you train physically, you're not just building strength or endurance. You're literally changing your brain. The chemicals released during movement boost your mood, sharpen focus, and wire in the habits that make mental control possible.

In Part 1 of this book, we'll discuss and examine:

1. How exercise primes the brain for learning and mental resilience
2. The long-term effects of physical training on focus, confidence, and stress regulation
3. Workouts that enhance, not just support, your mental performance as an archer
4. Different forms of exercise, how they benefit the archer, and workout plans to follow for each one of the various exercise modalities that you can start using immediately to become a stronger and more resilient athlete.

Part 2: Master the Inner Game

The second half of the book examines the core mental skills used by some of the best archers in the world. This isn't vague advice like, "trust the process," but a guide and a toolbox of proven strategies for improving your mental game to help you stay composed and execute under pressure.

These chapters will cover:

1. Visualization techniques to rehearse success
2. Mindfulness practices to train presence and process-oriented thinking
3. Self-talk and affirmations to reinforce confidence and consistency
4. Pressure training methods to inoculate yourself to manage performing under pressure better
5. How to build and refine pre-shot routines to make them more effective and consistent

Each concept in this book is backed by research, real-world examples, and drills and routines that you can integrate directly into your training.

Who This Book Is For

Whether you're new to archery, just developing or refining your shot, a collegiate archer, or a seasoned competitor seeking a competitive edge, this book is for you.

It's also for coaches who want to elevate their athletes, not just in score, but in maturity, focus, and personal growth. Mental strength, after all, transfers far beyond the range.

A New Standard for Archery Training

It's time to stop treating the mental game as mysterious or separate. It's not. Just as you train, over and over, to refine your form, you can develop and improve your mental performance if you break it down and train it with intention.

This book invites you to become a student of both mind and body, treating your nervous system as part of your gear, and to develop a process so strong that pressure becomes fuel rather than friction.

How to Use This Book

You'll get the most from this book if you treat it like a training manual, not just another archery book to read. Here's how:

1. Read with a pen and highlighter by your side. Take notes, underline ideas, and jot down your own insights.
2. Try the exercises. Each chapter contains practical routines, drills, and mental reps. Commit to practicing them over time before deciding if they work. In the same way our technical process takes time to develop and improve, our mental process needs the same attention.
3. Build your own systems. Utilize the templates and tools to develop a personalized technical and mental training plan that aligns with your training style and goals.

Come back often. Revisit chapters before a tournament, after a tough practice, or when your motivation needs a reset.

The Archer's Process

At the heart of this book is the belief that the most successful archers are not those who chase perfection; they are those who stick to a process. They aren't focused on outcomes, but on execution. They know how to respond when things go wrong because they have rehearsed, reflected, and refined both body and mind in training.

Now is your time.

PART I

CHAPTER 1

THE MENTAL DEMANDS OF ARCHERY

The uninitiated often misunderstand archery as a sport of physical dexterity and repetition alone. However, seasoned archers, coaches, and sports psychologists understand the more profound truth: archery is, to a great extent, a mental discipline. Precision in this sport is not from the body alone, but from the union of body and mind, with the mind often leading the way in determining success or failure.

The mental demands of archery are subtle but immeasurable, and they distinguish those who consistently achieve podium success from those who do not. In the following chapters and pages, we'll discuss the pressures, challenges, and mental patterns that govern high-performance archery. We'll also lay the foundation for understanding why physical training, far from being separate from the mental game, is one of the most powerful tools we have to shape it.

What Makes Archery a Mental Sport

The average person might assume that once you learn how to shoot a bow correctly, it's just a matter of repeating the process. Technically, they're right. The shot process doesn't fundamentally change from shot to shot, but what does change, often dramatically, is the internal experience of the archer.

When the stakes are low, like when we're having a relaxing practice on a calm day in our backyard while listening to our favorite music, most archers can shoot with a decent technical process. But introduce some pressure, a tournament, a head-to-head match, nearing a personal best, and everything changes. You can feel your heart rate increase, muscles tighten, and breathing becomes just a little faster. Your brain floods with thoughts: "They just shot a 10." "I can't miss this." "Everyone's watching." "What if I screw this up?"

Archery is one of the few sports in which the physical movement is relatively simple, while the mental and psychological complexity sits on the other end of the spectrum and can be extremely challenging. Executing your best shot under pressure requires an extraordinary level of mental discipline and control. The difference between a 10, 9, or 8 is often not in technique but in thought.

Olympians and Paralympians alike echo the same truth: they perform at just 80–90% of their full technical, scoring potential under pressure. The remaining 10–20% is often lost, usually not due to breakdown, but rather due to the mind's inability to remain calm and focused.

The mental game, then, is not just a part of archery; it is the test in which every arrow is measured.

Precision Requires Peace

Archery demands control, not just physical control, but mental control. When you draw the bow, muscles need to be active in the right places and relaxed in the others. The sight picture needs to be predictable but not frozen. The release should be deliberate but not forced. All of this happens best when your mind is focused.

Unfortunately, the mind is not quiet under pressure. Anxiety presents itself through the body: tension creeps into the shoulders, grip pressure increases, breathing becomes erratic, and shot timing speeds up or slows down unpredictably. One stray thought can throw off the entire process. If you think, even for a second, "Don't miss?", that thought can create a cascade of physical disruptions.

The best archers learn to cultivate a state of mental control. This doesn't mean the absence of thought; it means the presence of the RIGHT thoughts. Intentionally focused thoughts, or better yet, thoughts of presence, being entirely where you are, in the moment, within a shot. This is mindfulness in action, and later we'll cover a full chapter on this.

This ability to maintain internal focus in the face of external pressure is one of the defining characteristics of high-level competitors. And like all skills, it can be trained.

Performing Under Pressure

Pressure is the great amplifier. It doesn't create new problems; it magnifies the ones already present. An archer with a fragile mindset might perform well in practice, only to crumble when the stakes rise. This isn't because they forgot how to shoot. It's because pressure triggered a stress response in the brain and body.

When the brain perceives a threat (losing, embarrassment, or high expectations), it activates the sympathetic nervous system, which is your fight or flight response. This response is hardwired into human biology, our caveman brain, and while it's great for escaping predators, it's absolutely terrible for shooting a bow.

Under stress, your heart rate elevates. You may shake. Your vision narrows. Motor control deteriorates. These are not ideal conditions for executing a precise, technical movement. Pressure hijacks the prefrontal cortex, the part of your brain responsible for decision-making, emotional regulation, and working memory. This is why archers sometimes forget their shot process, skip a step, or panic mid-shot. The brain, in a moment of stress, temporarily short-circuits. As a young archer at my first indoor tournament, I dry-fired my bow and earned the nickname "Dry Fire" among my friends, which stuck with me for years. A process as simple as loading an arrow can be hijacked in the face of pressure.

The good news is that the brain can be trained to handle pressure. Exposure to competition and mindfulness training can improve the archer's ability to stay grounded in high-stress moments. We'll explore those tools in detail in Part II of this book. For now, it's important to understand that pressure isn't an enemy; it's a mirror that reflects your current level of mental preparation.

Focus, Consistency, and Present-Moment Awareness

The core of archery is repetition. Not just repeating the physical shot process, but repeating a mental process: focus, execute, evaluate, reset. This cycle is both mental and physical.

Focus is the gateway to consistency. Without focus, there is no repeatable performance, but focus is fragile. It can be disrupted by internal chatter, external noise, expectations, or even just the outcome of your last shot.

The consistent archer is one who learns to anchor their awareness in the present moment. Not the last arrow. Not the total score. Not what others are doing. Just THIS shot. Just THIS breath. Just THIS execution.

Mindfulness is the practice of intentionally directing attention without judgment. It is a powerful tool here. It helps the archer return to the present moment, again and again, no matter what has happened. When you develop an awareness of the present, you're more likely to respond to mistakes with interest rather than frustration. In these instances, you're more likely to stay centered even when things start heading in the wrong direction.

The path to mastery isn't about eliminating distractions forever; it's about minimizing the time between a distraction and your ability to refocus.

The Mind-Body Feedback Loop

One of the most critical insights in performance psychology is this: the body and the mind are not separate systems. They're deeply interwoven, constantly influencing one another.

When the body is calm and confident, it sends signals to the brain that everything is okay. When the body is tense and jittery, the brain interprets that as a sign of danger. The reverse is also true, if the brain is anxious, the body responds to match.

This feedback loop is always running. Successful archers learn to use it to their advantage. They recognize that controlling their breathing or body language can shift their internal thought process. They know that a few deep breaths can calm the nervous system. They understand that their self-talk affects their physical timing and tension.

The mind-body loop is the reason physical training is so powerful, not just for building strength or endurance, but also for enhancing mental clarity. As we'll see in the next chapter, exercise literally changes the chemistry of the brain, creating a mental environment that's more focused and confident.

A Mental Game Worth Training

Archery is not just about where the arrow lands. It's about HOW it got there. It's about what the archer was thinking, feeling, and focusing on. It's about whether their body was aligned with their intentions, and whether their mind was calm enough to allow their technical skills to surface.

The mental demands of archery are real and they're trainable. But they won't improve by accident. They improve with attention, intention, and deliberate practice.

In later chapters, we'll examine how physical training sharpens the mind. We'll see how exercise alters brain chemistry, how routines build consistency, and how you can elevate your mental performance through physical exercise. Then, we'll dive into the tools of the mental game: visualization, mindfulness, pressure training, and more.

For now, reflect on your own experience:

- When has your mind helped you shoot your best?
- When has it gotten in your way?
- What would your performance look like if your mind were always your ally?

CHAPTER 2

THE FOUNDATIONS OF PHYSICAL FITNESS FOR ARCHERS

Ask almost any archer, and they'll tell you archery is a mental sport. But here's something that often gets missed: your mind can't do its job well if your body isn't prepared. If you're physically exhausted, tense, or weak, no amount of mental game will make up for it. Physical preparation is what gives the mind the freedom to focus, stay calm, and perform under pressure. In this chapter, we're going to dig into how building a stronger, more balanced, and more durable body makes you a better archer, both physically and mentally.

Think about the last time you were tired, sore, or stiff during a long day of shooting. Chances are, it didn't just affect your body; it probably also messed with your focus, confidence, or self-talk. That's because the body and mind are connected. When one struggles, the other usually follows. But when your body feels strong, steady, and pain-free, your mind feels more in control.

Let's break this down into the three big pillars of archery fitness: strength, stability, and stamina. Each one supports your form, protects against injury, and frees your brain to focus on the things that win matches.

Strength: Control, Not Just Power

In archery, strength isn't about, "Hey bro, what do you bench?" It's about how well you can control and manage tension. It's being able to draw smoothly, hold, and execute without any extra or wasted movement. It seems that most coaches tend to think the muscles that matter most here are in the upper body, specifically the back and shoulders. This is simply inaccurate. Archery is a sport that requires the coordination of muscles in the lower, core, and upper body. It begins with your relationship with the ground. Most people are simply standing on the ground. I want you to be connected to the ground through the correct muscular activation. It begins with our toes, ends with the control of our head, and everything in between.

A strong, well-prepared body helps quiet the mind, leaving more capacity for mental performance. As researchers have pointed out, when movement becomes automatic through practice and repetition, your brain has more bandwidth for the mental side of performance. And strength training helps you get to that place faster, where your form is reliable enough that your mind can do what it does best: navigate you through high-pressure situations with focus and confidence.

Stability: The Foundation for Mental Poise

Mentally, stability builds trust. When your body feels strong and healthy, your brain doesn't have to check in constantly. That frees up mental bandwidth. You don't worry about whether your body is able to keep up; you can just shoot. And that trust in your body's ability creates a sense of calm. Confidence isn't a feeling that just appears; it comes from repetition, consistency, and knowing your body will show up when you need it most, because you've already put it to the test in training.

Stamina: The Ability to Outlast

Archery isn't a sprint. A single competition can last for hours, days, or even more than a week. Unofficial practice, official practice, qualification, head-to-head match play, team rounds, other delays, plus the heat, it all adds up. That's why stamina isn't just about physical energy. It's about being able to stay sharp, mentally and physically, even when your body starts to fade.

There are two kinds of stamina you need: aerobic and muscular. Aerobic stamina is developed through activities such as walking, running, hiking, or interval training. These build your base so your heart and lungs can keep your brain and muscles fueled with oxygen. It means you can shoot longer without getting tired or losing focus. Muscular endurance, meanwhile, is what lets you draw, hold, and execute again and again without a breakdown in form. This is where training for hypertrophy and volume-based strength sessions comes in handy.

And there's a third layer: mental endurance. When your body gets tired, your focus starts to fade. Decisions get slower, emotions feel heavier, and your discipline can waver. One powerful way to train all three simultaneously is to incorporate physical training into your shooting session. You'll be surprised how quickly you feel that physical fatigue in your mind. But that's the point. Training under mild fatigue helps you prepare for the moment in competition when your arms feel heavy, your breath is shallow, but you still need to execute.

Research by Hillman and others confirms what many coaches have observed firsthand: good cardiovascular fitness improves memory, emotional control, and decision-making. So when you feel a boost in your focus after a good training cycle, that's not just in your head. That's science at work.

The Mental Payoff of Physical Training

Here's the big picture: building your body builds your mind. Every tough workout teaches you resilience. Every time you show up sore and still put in the work, you reinforce mental toughness. That discipline carries directly into your shot process. The same mindset that gets you through a tough circuit is the one that gets you through a pressure-packed end.

When your body is strong, balanced, and pain-free, your mind doesn't have to fight it. That trust becomes your secret weapon. Confidence comes more easily. Flow shows up more often. You shoot with intention instead of fear or hesitation. And that's when your best happens, not because you forced them, but because you built the foundation they needed to appear.

Reflection Questions

1. How have physical issues like fatigue, muscle imbalances, or poor posture affected your consistency or confidence in past competitions?
2. Can you recall a time when being physically well-prepared made you feel more mentally focused or confident in your shooting? What contributed to that feeling?
3. What injury risks do you currently face (or have faced in the past), and what proactive steps can you take to reduce those risks moving forward?
4. What is one concrete goal you can set over the next month to improve your physical foundation in a way that will also benefit your mental performance?

CHAPTER 3

TRAIN YOUR BODY, TRAIN YOUR MIND

Every archer, whether beginner or elite, has experienced those moments of breakthrough when a technique finally clicks, when you feel a perfect shot, and your arrow hits the X. What we often don't realize is that this kind of progress isn't just physical, it's biological. Every adjustment we make, every improvement we feel, is rooted in learning.

But here's where it gets even more interesting: the process of learning can be accelerated. You can actually train your brain to become more efficient at acquiring skills, improving form, and processing feedback. And the key to doing this? Physical exercise.

Modern neuroscience is unraveling how exercise enhances learning, focus, memory, and plasticity. For archers, this means that one of the most powerful tools for skill development isn't just a bow.

This chapter explores the science of how exercise and movement shape the brain, how exercise impacts the rate and quality of learning, and how archers can apply this knowledge to improve faster.

The Science of Learning And How Exercise Changes the Game

Let's start by understanding that the brain is not fixed. It is constantly changing, adapting, and rewiring itself based on what we do and how we move. This phenomenon is called neuroplasticity, the brain's ability to change and adapt in response to experiences.

When we learn something new or rework what we already know, such as changing our hook or anchor position, we're not just processing instructions; we're altering the structure of our brain. Neurons fire together, form stronger connections, and physically change the shape and structure of brain circuits.

And this process doesn't just happen in a vacuum. It's enhanced by brain-derived neurotrophic factor (BDNF), which is a protein that supports the survival of existing neurons and encourages the growth of new ones. BDNF is like fertilizer for the brain, allowing it to grow, adapt, and wire new skills into memory.

So where does physical exercise come in?

Exercise is one of the most powerful triggers for BDNF production. Aerobic activity, in particular, floods the brain with BDNF, helping neurons grow, survive, and wire more efficiently. Think of a good exercise session as watering the garden of your brain, helping the seeds of skill and knowledge that you planted take root and grow.

Numerous studies have confirmed this. Mice that exercised regularly grew significantly more new neurons in the hippocampus, the brain's learning and memory center, compared to sedentary mice. And in humans, just one bout of moderate exercise improved learning speed, vocabulary acquisition, and cognitive flexibility.

Your Brain on Exercise

Beyond BDNF, exercise has a profound effect on neurotransmitters, the brain's chemical messengers. Movement increases the production and balance of serotonin, dopamine, norepinephrine, and endorphins. Each of these plays a vital role in learning:

Serotonin improves mood and emotional control, helping you stay positive and resilient during tough training cycles.

Dopamine enhances motivation, reward sensitivity, and the "feel-good" sensation we associate with progress.

Norepinephrine sharpens focus, alertness, and reaction time.

Endorphins reduce pain and increase well-being, helping you stay engaged even when training gets hard.

This chemical cocktail is powerful for an archer. We often talk about the mental game, staying composed under pressure, managing nerves, maintaining focus, all those things, and more, but we forget that these mental skills are deeply physiological. Exercise can help you prepare your brain to focus when you need it most.

Why Fit Archers Learn Faster

In a landmark study, German researchers found that participants learned vocabulary words 20% faster after exercise. Another study demonstrated that people who exercised regularly showed enhanced brain plasticity and better memory retention compared to sedentary individuals. The implication? If you're in good physical shape, you learn better and faster.

This is huge for archery, where success depends on skill acquisition, precision, and consistency. Each shot repeats a mental and physical motor program. Exercise enhances this process by increasing blood flow, stimulating neurotransmitter release, and flooding the brain with BDNF. It helps you learn new techniques faster and retain them longer.

The Motor Learning Connection: Mind, Muscle, and Movement

Archery is both a fine motor skill and a full-body coordination task. The shot process depends on precise activation of the posterior chain, shoulder stabilization, core engagement, and the ability to execute the shot, all orchestrated through the brain's motor centers.

When you exercise, especially in ways that challenge coordination, balance, or agility, you activate the cerebellum and motor cortex, both of which are essential for controlling movement and learning new motor sequences.

Even more fascinating, exercise creates a feedback loop between the cerebellum and the prefrontal cortex (which is responsible for decision-making, planning, and conscious thought). This connection supports complex motor learning, like adapting your shot while aiming off shooting in the wind.

Training Breaks

Many archers approach training as a grind: hour after hour on the line, drilling form. But neuroscience suggests that breaking up your technical sessions with aerobic movement or strength training could actually accelerate your improvement.

Movement does more than just wake you up. It increases oxygen to the brain, enhances memory formation, and primes the brain's learning circuits.

Consider testing the following movement strategies in the middle of your training sessions. Be sure to take time to reflect on whether incorporating exercise in the middle of training was beneficial.

- **Practice Cardio Break:** 5-10 minutes of light aerobic exercise improves blood flow and BDNF release.
- **Mid-Session Movement Breaks:** Instead of grinding through a session, take a 5-minute break to take a short walk.
- **Post-Practice Reflection Walks:** Gentle walking after a session improves session reflection and memory.

Exercise and Mental Resilience

Learning requires some level of grit, emotional regulation, and resilience, especially in archery, where small failures are constant.

Exercise enhances the brain's ability to manage stress by regulating the hypothalamic-pituitary-adrenal (HPA) axis, the system responsible for releasing cortisol, the stress hormone. Regular physical activity trains this system to be less reactive, so you're less likely to spiral into negative thinking after a poor shot.

Even more compelling, studies show that fit individuals have more robust connectivity between brain regions responsible for emotional control. In other words, the more you exercise, the better equipped you are to handle frustration, learn from failure, and reset quickly.

The Learning Trifecta

Let's zoom in on three key players:

1. Neurogenesis is the birth of new brain cells.
2. BDNF is the protein that supports those cells.
3. The hippocampus is the region where it all comes together.

When you exercise, you stimulate the creation of new neurons in the hippocampus. But those neurons don't last long unless they're given a job. Learning gives them that job. The more you learn while those neurons are active, the stronger your memory becomes.

This means that combining exercise with learning, whether through practice, drills, journaling, or coaching review, is not just helpful. It's optimal. You're literally growing the brain infrastructure required to retain what you're practicing.

When the Brain is Most Receptive

High-intensity exercise redirects blood flow away from the prefrontal cortex, which temporarily reduces executive function. That's why trying to absorb complex feedback while maxed out on heart rate isn't effective.

But once your workout ends and blood flow returns to normal, your brain enters a window of heightened ability. This "afterglow" lasts for about 30 to 60 minutes and is the ideal time for:

- Reflective journaling
- Watching video footage of your form
- Receiving technical coaching cues
- Practicing new drills
- Visualization and mental rehearsal (which we cover in Part II of this book)

Schedule your learning tasks for this window and watch how much more effective your training becomes.

Skill Retention, Pattern Recognition, and the Power of Practice

When exercise primes the brain, it enhances not just short-term learning but also skill retention. You don't just learn faster, you forget slower.

Exercise also improves pattern recognition. Whether you're reading the wind, aiming off, or making sight adjustments, recognizing subtle patterns in your environment or body is key to elite performance.

Exercise improves executive function and reaction time, supporting the ability to scan, assess, and respond with precision.

Exercise, Learn, Master

Archery is more than a game of muscle memory. Science now supports the idea that when you train your body, you train your mind.

You don't have to choose between physical training and skill work. When done with intention, they amplify each other. So the next time you're lacing up for a run or preparing for a workout, remember that you're not just building muscle. You're building, refining, and improving the mental game that we talk so much about.

Reflection Questions

1. What is your warm-up like before practice, and could you use that time more intentionally to prime your brain?
2. How might adding 10–15 minutes of aerobic activity before practice change your focus or performance?
3. Do you schedule time for reflection or visualization after your workouts or practice?
4. If not, how might you use the "afterglow window" of enhanced neuroplasticity to review what you've learned?
5. Have you ever struggled to retain a new skill or technique?
6. Could it be that your brain wasn't in an optimal state for learning at the time? What might you change about your physical state before attempting difficult technical changes again?

7. What's one small, consistent change you can make starting this week to integrate more brain-enhancing movement into your archery training?
8. Write it down and commit to trying it for the next 7 days.

CHAPTER 4

WARMUP AND MOBILITY

One of the most overlooked elements of performance is how you prepare your body to shoot. At your next tournament, take a few seconds to look around and see it for yourself. You'll see that most archers are just not warming up prior to competition. The fact is that most archers step onto the range without a warmup and assume that their first few arrows are a good enough warmup, but this increases the risk of injury and stalls both mental and physical performance. But an intentional, well designed warm-up primes both body and mind to prepare you to shoot at your best.

Why Warming Up Matters for Archers

Archery is a repetitive sport that places significant strain on the shoulders, upper back, and core. A proper warm-up addresses these issues before they cause problems. It increases blood flow, elevates muscle temperature, and prepares your nervous system for stability. In addition to the physical benefits, warm-ups also fuel your mental game.

Research supports using warm-ups to enhance physical readiness and cognitive performance. Even a short warm-up of 10-15 minutes can significantly improve motor control, coordination, and attention. In addition, studies have shown that 5–10 minutes of aerobic activity increases blood flow to the brain, enhancing alertness, reaction time, and mood. This mind-body connection is what elevates performance.

Key Components of an Effective Archery Warm-Up

1. General Movement (3–5 minutes) Start with light cardio to raise your core temperature. Exercises in this category can include:

- Arm circles and swings
- Jumping jacks
- Jogging or jumping in place
- Shoulder rolls and shrugs

2. Dynamic Mobility (5–8 minutes) Next, move through a range of motion that mimics shooting. Exercises in this category can include:

- ⊠ **oracic Rotations:** Kneeling or standing, twist gently from side to side to loosen your spine.
- **World's Greatest Stretch:** A compound stretch that opens hips, spine, and shoulders.
- **Scapular Push-Ups:** Activate the shoulder blades and chest in a push-up position with protraction/retraction.

3. Targeted Activation (5–10 minutes) Now focus on the muscles that help stabilize your shot:

- **Band Pull-Aparts:** Strengthen the mid-back and rear deltoids.
- **Face Pulls with Bands:** Retrain scapular retraction and shoulder alignment.
- **Y-T-Ws:** Low-resistance band or bodyweight movements to prep the rotator cuff.
- **Wall Slides:** Improve shoulder blade mechanics against a flat surface.

Sample 10–15 Minute Warm-Up Circuit for Archers

Warm-ups should generally be performed in a continuous flow, with little to no rest between movements. This keeps the body warm, increases heart rate, and elevates focus. However, short transitions of 10–15 seconds between movements are perfectly fine and are totally acceptable, especially when shifting from one type of exercise to another, like mobility to band work. The key is to avoid a long rest period during the warmup that interrupts physiological readiness. Your warm-up should be a light physical challenge, nothing too crazy where rest is needed.

In terms of RPE (Rate of Perceived Exertion), your warm-up should fall around a 3 out of 10. Again, this is just a light challenge to get you warm and mentally engaged but not fatigued. The goal is activation, not exhaustion. You want to finish the warm-up feeling sharper and more mobile than when you started, not rundown and exhausted.

Below is a sample warm-up routine. Again, this is just a sample. In order to stay consistent in all settings, your warm-up routine should be something you enjoy and are comfortable performing at home, at your local club, and at tournaments.

1. Jumping Jacks – 1 minute
2. Thoracic Rotations – 1 minute
3. Arm Swings – 1 minute
4. Band Pull-Aparts – 2 sets of 10
5. Banded Over Unders – 2 sets of 10
6. Banded Y-T-Ws – 1 set of each (8 reps each)
7. Banded Draw, Hold and Anchor– 2 sets of 5 reps

Integrating SPTs: Specific Physical Training for Archery

A highly effective way to complement your warm-up routine and build archery-specific strength is through SPTs, Specific Physical Training. Originally popularized by recurve programs, particularly in Korea, SPTs are now widely adopted by competitive archers around the world. These exercises simulate aspects of the shot cycle to build strength, endurance, and mental resilience.

Types of SPTs:

- **Holding SPT:** Draw to full anchor and hold for 10-20 seconds, then let down. Repeat for multiple reps. This builds isometric shoulder and scapular strength, which supports aiming and steadiness under pressure.
- **Repetition SPT:** Repeatedly draw and let down without releasing, 10 to 15 reps, focusing on consistency and

control. This refines movement and builds muscular endurance.

- **Full Shot SPT:** Shoot high-volume blank bale arrows, often in structured sets, to reinforce perfect form and condition your mind-body system to sustain peak execution.

Why Use SPTs?

SPTs develop the very muscle groups you rely on to shoot while reinforcing your technique under fatigue. They also train your mind to stay calm and focused when tired, mirroring competition stress. For archers looking to build baseline strength, SPTs offer a low impact addition to other training programs which are discussed in later chapters.

You can incorporate SPTs 2-4 times per week, either as part of a warm-up or as their own short workout. Start with 2-3 sets of holding drills, gradually increasing duration and volume as strength improves.

When to Warm Up Before Shooting

If shooting begins at 8:00 a.m., archers should plan to begin their warm-up routine around 7:30 to 7:40 a.m. This allows time for a 10-15-minute warm-up, a short transition period, and any final equipment preparation before stepping to the line. The goal is to complete the warm-up close enough to benefit from its physiological and psychological effects, but not so close that you feel rushed or have to start shooting in a fatigued state.

After warming up, take a short 5-10 minute break before shooting. Use this time to hydrate, mentally rehearse, or double-check gear, which can help solidify the mental transition from prep to performance. Archers should feel warm, focused, and relaxed as they approach their first shot.

Consistency Between Practice and Competition

To maximize effectiveness, archers should aim to develop a consistent warm-up routine that they use before both practice and competition. By sticking to a familiar warm-up, archers send clear signals to their brain and body that it's time to perform. The warm-up becomes a ritualized transition from an everyday mindset to competitive readiness. When that routine is practiced regularly, it enhances confidence, even in high-pressure environments.

CHAPTER 5

CHOOSING YOUR TRAINING PATH

Laying the Groundwork

Before we jump into the four different training chapters and programs most beneficial for archers, Cardiovascular Conditioning, Muscular Endurance, Hypertrophy, and High-Intensity Interval Training, it's important to understand that you don't need to do all of them. In fact, you shouldn't, at least not all at once.

The goal of this section is to help you choose one training style that fits your body, your archery goals, and your lifestyle. You'll get the best results by sticking with one well-structured plan, performed consistently and with intention. These programs aren't meant to be mixed and matched. Each one is a complete system, designed to progressively challenge your body and sharpen your mind in a specific way.

So how do you decide which one is right for you?

That decision starts with understanding what each program is built to do:

- **Cardiovascular Conditioning** builds your aerobic engine, improves endurance, fatigue resistance, and sharpens mental stamina.
- **Muscular Endurance** improves your ability to maintain form and stability under fatigue, key for long days of shooting and high-pressure situations.
- **Hypertrophy Training** focuses on building lean muscle and developing a strong, stable foundation through targeted resistance work.
- **High-Intensity Interval Training (HIIT)** is a time-efficient way to build work capacity, improve recovery, and sharpen mental toughness through short bursts of intensity.

In the chapters ahead, you'll learn the ins and outs of each of these programs. But before you dive into the one that resonates with you most, let's talk about the common training language and core concepts you'll see throughout this section.

Supersets: Pairing Movements for Maximum Efficiency

A superset is when you perform two exercises back-to-back without resting in between. Usually, these exercises target different muscle groups (like biceps and triceps, or legs and shoulders). Supersets save time and increase the intensity of your workout. They're especially useful in muscular endurance and hypertrophy workouts where maintaining a training rhythm is key.

Why it matters for archers: Supersets help you build both physical and mental resilience. They keep your body moving and your focus sharp without the long pauses that can cool your momentum.

Giant Sets: Going All In

A giant set is similar to a superset, but with three or more exercises performed in sequence with little to no rest. Think of it as a circuit focused on one area (like shoulders) or a full-body blitz that challenges your coordination, endurance, and grit. Giant sets are great for high-rep muscular endurance, hypertrophy and HIIT-style workouts.

Why it matters for archers: Giant sets push your limits and simulate the kind of fatigue you might feel in a long tournament or back-to-back matches.

Primers: Waking Up the Right Muscles

A primer is a short, low-intensity exercise or series of movements done before your main workout. It's designed to wake up key muscles, improve neuromuscular activation, and prepare your body for the work ahead.

Why it matters for archers: Priming the right muscles ensures you're not just warming up; you're getting your nervous system dialed in for precise movement, which directly transfers to better shot execution.

Time Under Tension: Feel the Burn

Time under tension (TUT) refers to how long your muscles are under strain during a set. In hypertrophy training, slowing down the tempo of your reps increases TUT, which leads to more muscle growth and better muscle-mind connection.

Why it matters for archers: Learning to move slowly and under control teaches your body to hold tension, stabilize joints, and resist fatigue.

Progressive Overload: The Secret to Results

Progressive overload is the principle of gradually increasing the stress placed on your body during training. That might mean lifting heavier weights, doing more reps, increasing time under tension, or reducing rest periods. The key is to challenge your body just a little more over time.

Why it matters for archers: Whether you're trying to build strength, endurance, or control, progress only happens if your body is nudged slightly out of its comfort zone. This principle is a part of every program you'll find in this book.

Rest Periods

How long you rest between sets depends on the training style you're following:

- Cardiovascular Conditioning: Minimal rest; work is continuous or interval-based with active recovery.

- Muscular Endurance: 30 to 60 seconds between sets, just enough to catch your breath but not fully recover.
- Hypertrophy Training: 60 to 90 seconds between sets. This balance allows for partial recovery without losing the muscle-building stimulus.
- HIIT: Variable, intense work followed by structured rest, as noted in the workout, designed to elevate heart rate and simulate performance bursts.

Why it matters for archers: Rest periods influence how your body adapts. Shorter rests train you to recover quickly, while longer rests allow for more strength and power in each set. Choose the rest that matches your goal.

Mind-Muscle Connection: Train With Intention

The mind-muscle connection is your ability to focus on the muscle you're using during a movement. Research shows that consciously engaging a muscle (instead of just "going through the motions") leads to better activation and more effective training.

Why it matters for archers: This concept mirrors how you practice archery, being intentional with each rep, staying tuned into your form, and feeling each movement. Training with awareness improves both physical results and mental sharpness.

One Path, One Focus

There's no "best" program, only the one that's best for you right now.

- If your main issue is fatigue during tournaments, cardiovascular conditioning might be your path.
- If your body breaks down late in the day or your muscles fatigue in competition, muscular endurance could be the game-changer.
- If you want to build strength, structure, and stability, hypertrophy is what you're looking for.
- If you thrive on intensity and want to push your mental and physical limits, HIIT might be for you.

Whatever path you choose, stick with it. Give it at least 4–6 consistent weeks before re-evaluating and moving to another program. Trust the process and let it do its job.

You don't need to be perfect. You just need to be consistent, intentional, and committed to your growth. In the next chapters, we'll break down each training style in detail so you can begin your journey with confidence.

Reflection Questions:

1. What is the biggest performance issue you currently face in archery?
2. Which training style feels the most aligned with your goals and personality?
3. Are you more motivated by structure, intensity, variety, or steady progress?
4. What time and equipment do you have access to right now?
5. Are you willing to commit to one style of training for at least 4–6 weeks?

CHAPTER 6

CARDIOVASCULAR CONDITIONING

When most archers think about training, their minds jump to the muscles of the upper body that support the draw cycle, holding, and shot execution. Rarely do they consider how a strong heart and efficient lungs impact performance. Additionally, cardiovascular conditioning lays the foundation for mental performance, control, and resilience across long tournaments and pressure scenarios. Good cardio conditioning doesn't just improve your recovery between ends; it strengthens your ability to stay calm under pressure, regulate breathing during your shot process, and maintain focus when others start to fade. Whether you're new to cardiovascular conditioning or have completed numerous marathons, there's a beginner, intermediate, and advanced program in this chapter to suit your needs and strengthen your mind.

Beginner Cardio Plan Week 1

Workout 1

20 min walk + 30 sec jog x3

This workout starts with a steady walk, and three times during the walk you'll do a 30-second light jog. Begin with a warm-up walk for 5 minutes. Then, jog for 30 seconds, followed by 3–5 minutes of walking to recover. Repeat that jog two more times throughout the 20 minutes. This helps you ease into the feeling of jogging without overexerting yourself.

Workout 2

25 min steady walk

This is a simple, steady-paced walk for 25 minutes. The goal is to maintain a consistent, comfortable pace that lets you breathe easily and stay relaxed. It's an easy day meant to build endurance and reinforce the habit of movement.

Workout 3

20 min walk + 30 sec jog x4

You'll complete four short 30-second jogs during this 20-minute walk. Warm up by walking for 5 minutes, then jog for 30 seconds. Recover by walking for a few minutes, then repeat the jog three more times. End the session with walking to complete your 20 minutes.

Beginner Cardio Plan Week 2

Workout 1

20 min walk + 45 sec jog x3

This session includes three 45-second jogs spaced throughout a 20-minute walk. Start with a 5-minute walk to warm up. Then jog for 45 seconds and walk for 3–5 minutes to recover. Repeat the jog two more times, and finish by walking until you've reached the 20-minute mark.

Workout 2

25 min steady walk

Go for a steady, comfortable walk lasting 25 minutes. You should feel like you're moving with purpose, but not so fast that you can't talk comfortably. This recovery-style workout helps you stay active while giving your body a break from jogging.

Workout 3

20 min walk + 45 sec jog x5

This workout includes five short jogs lasting 45 seconds each. Begin with a warm-up walk, then jog for 45 seconds followed by 2–3 minutes of walking. Repeat the jog five times total and walk in between to recover and complete your 20-minute session.

Beginner Cardio Plan Week 3

Workout 1

20 min walk + 1 min jog x4

You'll do four 1-minute jogs during your 20-minute walk. Start with 5 minutes of walking, then alternate between 1 minute of jogging and 3 minutes of walking to recover. Repeat this four times and walk to fill in any remaining time.

Workout 2

30 min steady walk

Take a consistent, steady-paced walk for 30 minutes. This session focuses on endurance and gives your body a break from higher-intensity work. Keep your pace strong but comfortable.

Workout 3

20 min walk + 1 min jog x6

You'll complete six 1-minute jogs during this 20-minute session. Begin with a warm-up walk, then alternate between jogging for 1 minute and walking for 2–3 minutes. Repeat the jogs six times and continue walking to complete the full 20 minutes.

Beginner Cardio Plan Week 4

Workout 1

25 min walk + 90 sec jog x4

This workout includes four 90-second jogs. Start with a warm-up walk, then jog for 90 seconds. Walk for about 3 minutes to recover, and repeat the jogs four times total. Continue walking to complete 25 minutes.

Workout 2

30 min steady walk

Take a steady walk for 30 minutes, focusing on posture, breathing, and rhythm. This workout promotes recovery and builds endurance at a lower intensity.

Workout 3

25 min walk + 90 sec jog x5

Do five 90-second jogs during your 25-minute walk. Begin with a walk to warm up, then jog and recover by walking for 2–3 minutes in between each jog. Repeat the pattern five times and walk to fill out the 25-minute session.

Beginner Cardio Plan Week 5

Workout 1

30 min brisk walk/jog mix

This workout gives you freedom to mix jogging and brisk walking over 30 minutes. After a warm-up, alternate between 1–2 minutes of jogging and 3–4 minutes of brisk walking, or use your own intervals depending on how you feel. The idea is to keep moving and let your body guide the effort.

Workout 2

30 min steady walk

Take a 30-minute walk at a consistent pace. This session is meant to be low-intensity but steady, helping you recover from the jog-focused workouts while still maintaining cardiovascular progress.

Workout 3

30 min walk + 2 min jog x4

Complete four 2-minute jogs throughout your 30-minute session. Start with a warm-up, then jog for 2 minutes followed by 3 minutes of walking. Repeat the jogs four times and walk in between to recover and complete the workout.

Beginner Cardio Plan Week 6

Workout 1

30 min jog/walk intervals

This session combines jogging and walking intervals based on how you feel. Begin with a 5-minute walk, then alternate jogging for 1–2 minutes with walking for 1–3 minutes. Repeat these intervals until you've reached 30 minutes total. Adjust the jog-to-walk ratio as needed to keep moving comfortably.

Workout 2

30 min brisk walk

Take a brisk-paced walk for 30 minutes. This should feel more energetic than a normal walk. Swing your arms naturally, stay tall through your posture, and focus on maintaining your pace from start to finish.

Workout 3

35 min continuous walk or jog

This final workout gives you the choice to walk, jog, or combine both. Your goal is to stay in motion for a full 35 minutes. If you're able to jog for longer periods, go for it! If not, alternate as needed. This is the last step in your beginner program, so enjoy the progress you've made.

Intermediate Cardio Plan Week 1

Workout 1

3 × 5-minute jog, 2-minute walk

Jog for five minutes at a steady pace, then walk for two minutes to recover. Repeat this jog-walk pattern three times. This workout helps ease into longer jogging segments with short walking breaks.

Workout 2

25-minute steady jog

Jog continuously for 25 minutes at a comfortable, sustainable pace. This is a steady effort, slow enough to maintain, but not so easy that it feels like a walk.

Workout 3

30-minute walk/jog mix

During this 30-minute session, alternate between walking and jogging however you feel comfortable. Try to keep jogging for 1–2 minutes at a time with walking breaks in between. This workout gives you flexibility while encouraging continuous movement.

Workout 4

4 × 3-minute jog, 90-second walk

Jog for three minutes, then walk for 90 seconds to recover. Repeat this four times. This workout builds stamina with slightly shorter intervals to focus on maintaining good form.

Intermediate Cardio Plan Week 2

Workout 1

4 × 5-minute jog, 2-minute walk

Jog for five minutes, then walk for two minutes to recover. Repeat this four times. This adds one extra interval compared to Week 1 and helps you build endurance gradually.

Workout 2

30-minute steady jog

Jog for a continuous 30 minutes at a consistent, moderate pace. You should be able to speak in short phrases but not carry on a full conversation.

Workout 3

30-minute jog/walk intervals

Alternate between jogging and walking for 30 minutes. Try jogging for 2–3 minutes at a time, followed by walking for 1–2 minutes. Choose a rhythm that challenges you but still feels manageable.

Workout 4

4 × 4-minute jog, 1-minute walk

Jog for four minutes, then walk for one minute. Repeat this four times. These shorter walks help you learn how to recover quickly and build up to longer jogging durations.

Intermediate Cardio Plan Week 3

Workout 1

3 × 8-minute jog, 90-second walk

Jog for eight minutes, then take a 90-second walking break. Repeat this three times. These longer jogging blocks build mental and physical endurance.

Workout 2

35-minute steady jog

Run for 35 minutes at a steady, relaxed pace. You're not racing, just aiming to stay consistent the entire time. This is a key workout to develop base aerobic fitness.

Workout 3

30-minute jog + 4 × 30-second strides

Jog continuously for 30 minutes at an easy pace. After the jog, do four short "strides." These are 30-second controlled sprints or faster-paced runs, followed by a walk or rest. Focus on form and speed during the strides.

Workout 4

4 × 5-minute jog, 1-minute walk

Jog for five minutes and walk for one minute. Repeat this four times. It's a return to shorter, more comfortable blocks to help you recover from the week's longer efforts.

Intermediate Cardio Plan Week 4

Workout 1

2 × 10-minute jog, 2-minute walk

Jog for 10 minutes, walk for 2 minutes to recover, and repeat the 10-minute jog one more time. These long intervals help prepare you for continuous running with short walking breaks for recovery.

Workout 2

40-minute steady jog

Jog at a steady, manageable pace for a full 40 minutes. This is your longest steady jog so far, aimed at building confidence in your ability to maintain a rhythm over time.

Workout 3

30-minute recovery jog

This is a light, easy-paced 30-minute jog. The goal here is to help your body recover from the previous harder workouts while still keeping your legs moving.

Workout 4

5 × 4-minute jog, 1-minute walk

Jog for four minutes, walk for one minute, and repeat five times. These intervals provide structure while letting you build volume without overexerting yourself.

Intermediate Cardio Plan Week 5

Workout 1

3 × 10-minute jog, 1-minute walk

Jog for 10 minutes, walk for 1 minute, and repeat that cycle three times. You're spending more time jogging with very short recovery walks, this is a great endurance builder.

Workout 2

45-minute steady jog

Jog at a consistent pace for 45 minutes. Don't worry about speed, just focus on finishing the time. This long run develops both mental toughness and cardiovascular strength.

Workout 3

30-minute jog + 6 strides

Jog continuously for 30 minutes at an easy pace. Afterward, complete six 30-second strides, short bursts of faster running with a focus on smooth, efficient form. Walk or rest between strides.

Workout 4

4 × 6-minute jog, 90-second walk

Jog for six minutes, walk for 90 seconds, and repeat four times. This moderate interval length bridges the gap between shorter efforts and your long jogs.

Intermediate Cardio Plan Week 6

Workout 1

40-minute steady jog

Jog for 40 minutes at a smooth, steady pace. This is a solid effort to maintain your fitness and rhythm as you finish out the final week.

Workout 2

50-minute long jog

Jog continuously for 50 minutes, the longest effort of the program. Keep your pace relaxed, focus on consistency, and take short walking breaks only if needed.

Workout 3

20-minute recovery jog

Take this day easy with a slow-paced 20-minute jog. You should feel like you're just shaking the legs out, no pushing or intensity here.

Workout 4

3 × 8-minute jog, 1-minute walk

Jog for eight minutes, walk for one minute, and repeat that cycle three times. This wraps up your plan with strong, sustained efforts and short walking breaks for recovery.

Advanced Cardio Plan Week 1

Workout 1

30-minute tempo run

Run for 30 minutes at a "comfortably hard" pace, faster than a jog, but sustainable without gasping for air. You should be able to speak only in short phrases. Tempo runs improve your ability to hold a faster pace and increase your lactate threshold.

Workout 2

45-minute aerobic base run

Jog or run at a steady, moderate pace for 45 minutes. This pace should be easy enough to talk through. The goal is to build aerobic endurance without pushing intensity.

Workout 3

30-minute easy jog

Jog at a relaxed pace for 30 minutes. This is a recovery workout, meant to keep your legs loose without adding stress. Keep things light and conversational.

Workout 4

6 × 400m (or 90-second) intervals

Complete six intervals, each either 400 meters or 90 seconds of fast running, followed by a walk or slow jog to recover (1–2 minutes).

These short, quick efforts improve speed, turnover, and running form under intensity.

Workout 5

60-minute long run

Run for a full hour at a relaxed, steady pace. Focus on pacing yourself early so you can maintain your effort through the full duration. Long runs are the foundation of endurance building.

Advanced Cardio Plan Week 2

Workout 1

4 × 6-minute intervals, 2-minute jog recovery

Run hard for six minutes, then jog slowly for two minutes to recover. Repeat four times. These longer intervals develop stamina and simulate race-like effort levels.

Workout 2

50-minute aerobic base run

Run for 50 minutes at a moderate, comfortable pace. This is about getting time on your feet and building endurance without taxing your system.

Workout 3

30-minute easy jog + strides

Go for an easy 30-minute jog. At the end, complete four to six 20–30 second strides, short bursts of faster running focused on good form, not sprinting.

Workout 4

6 × 90-second fast, 90-second jog

Alternate between 90 seconds of fast running and 90 seconds of slow jogging for recovery. Repeat this cycle six times. This type of interval trains both speed and recovery.

Workout 5

65-minute long run

Jog or run for 65 minutes at a steady pace. This session reinforces endurance and builds your aerobic base, so focus on pacing and staying relaxed.

Advanced Cardio Plan Week 3

Workout 1

35-minute tempo run

Run at a tempo pace, comfortably hard but sustainable for 35 minutes. You're not sprinting, but you should feel like you're working. This run improves endurance and speed control.

Workout 2

55-minute aerobic base run

Complete a 55-minute steady-paced run. Keep things aerobic, meaning you should still be able to talk in full sentences without breathlessness.

Workout 3

30-minute recovery jog

Jog at a very light and easy pace for 30 minutes. This run helps your muscles recover while maintaining consistency in your training week.

Workout 4

4 × 5-minute intervals, 90-second jog

Run hard for five minutes, followed by a 90-second jog to recover. Repeat four times. This type of effort boosts speed endurance and teaches your body how to recover efficiently.

Workout 5

70-minute long run

Jog or run continuously for 70 minutes at a relaxed pace. Keep your breathing steady, focus on posture, and settle into a rhythm. This is a key weekly run for endurance.

Advanced Cardio Plan Week 4

Workout 1

6 × 3-minute fast, 2-minute jog

Complete six sets of 3-minute fast running intervals, each followed by 2 minutes of light jogging for recovery. These shorter but intense efforts help with speed, leg turnover, and running efficiency.

Workout 2

50-minute aerobic run

Go for a 50-minute steady-state run. Keep it at a pace that feels natural and aerobic, not too hard, not too easy. This builds cardiovascular endurance.

Workout 3

35-minute easy jog + strides

Jog for 35 minutes at an easy pace. Afterward, perform four to six short strides of 20–30 seconds each. Focus on relaxed form and smooth acceleration.

Workout 4

5 × hill sprints (45 seconds)

Find a moderate hill and sprint up it for 45 seconds. Walk back down to recover fully, then repeat five times. This develops strength, power, and explosive mechanics.

Workout 5

75-minute long run

Run for 75 minutes at a relaxed, steady pace. This is your longest run yet, focus on managing your energy and keeping consistent throughout the entire distance.

Advanced Cardio Plan Week 5

Workout 1

40-minute tempo progression run

Start at a steady pace, and gradually increase your speed every 10 minutes until the final block feels like your tempo pace. This teaches you to control pace, increase effort gradually, and finish strong.

Workout 2

55-minute aerobic base run

Run for 55 minutes at a moderate, conversational pace. This workout continues building aerobic capacity and reinforces consistent endurance work.

Workout 3

30-minute recovery jog

Jog lightly for 30 minutes. This easy session helps your legs recover while maintaining your routine. Focus on relaxed effort and fluid motion.

Workout 4

6 × 2-minute fast, 2-minute jog

Alternate between two minutes of faster running and two minutes of jogging for recovery. Repeat this pattern six times. This workout mixes speed and recovery into one balanced session.

Workout 5

80-minute long run

Run for 80 minutes at a relaxed pace. These long runs teach your body to become more fuel-efficient and mentally tough, key for distance performance.

Advanced Cardio Plan Week 6

Workout 1

3 × 10-minute intervals, 2-minute jog

Run at a strong, controlled pace for 10 minutes, then jog slowly for two minutes. Repeat this cycle three times. These long intervals simulate race pace and teach sustainable effort.

Workout 2

60-minute steady run

Run continuously for an hour at a steady, moderate pace. You should feel strong and in control, not pushing, but not slacking either.

Workout 3

35-minute easy jog + 6 strides

Jog for 35 minutes at a relaxed pace. Finish the run with six strides of about 30 seconds each, with walking or standing rest in between. These help sharpen your legs without tiring you out.

Workout 4

20-minute fartlek (alternating fast/slow pace)

During this 20-minute run, alternate between short bursts of faster running and slower jogging. You can vary the timing, such as 1 minute fast, 1 minute slow. The purpose is to train speed variation and responsiveness.

Workout 5

85–90-minute long run

This is your longest run of the plan, go for 85 to 90 minutes at a steady, aerobic pace. Focus on staying relaxed, fueling as needed, and maintaining good posture. This run caps off your six weeks with a strong foundation of endurance and confidence.

CHAPTER 7

MUSCULAR ENDURANCE

Muscular endurance is the key to staying strong and maintaining your form deep into a long round, resisting breakdown in technique, and keeping execution crisp when others start to lose it. It's what allows an archer to shoot well, even after hours of shooting or during the final ends of a high-stakes match. But muscular endurance is more than just physical stamina; it's mental grit in motion. Training for muscular endurance conditions both body and brain to stay composed and sharp through discomfort. In this chapter, you'll be presented with a well-rounded training program for muscular endurance that will set you up with the resilience to finish every shot as strong as the first. Whether you're new to the gym or a seasoned professional, there's a beginner, intermediate, and advanced program in this chapter to suit your needs and sharpen your mind.

Beginner 3-Day Muscular Endurance Plan

Week 1, Day 1 – Full Body Foundation

This workout kicks off your muscular endurance plan by building a foundation of stamina across your entire body. With higher reps and controlled form, you're training your muscles to resist fatigue, perfect for archers who need to shoot and maintain form for hours. Focus on movement quality and controlled breathing. Today's session activates all major muscle groups, setting the tone for resilience and improved muscular efficiency.

Notes	Exercise	Sets/Reps
	Week 1, Day 1	
	Lying Hamstring Curl	3 x 20,15,12
	Squat, Leg Press, Hack Squat or Smith Squat	3 x 10-12
	Hip Thrust	2 x 15
	Push - Flat Machine Chest Press, BB or DB	3 x 20,15,12
	Pull - Chest Supported Row Machine or Cable Row, BB or DB	3 x 15,12,10
	Vertical Push - Machine Shoulder Press	2 x 12-15
	Vertical Pull - Lat Pulldown	2 x 12-15

Week 1, Day 2 – Shoulders and Arms for Stability

Today, we zero in on shoulders and arms. Endurance in these areas means a steadier hold and fewer breakdowns in form late in a tournament. High-volume shoulder and tricep work can help prevent fatigue-induced form collapse. Keep reps clean and deliberate, aiming to feel the burn without rushing through.

Notes	Exercise	Sets/Reps
	Week 1 - Day 2	
	DB Walking Lunges	3 x 12
	DB Shoulder Press	3 x 15
	Lying Hamstring Curl	3 x 15
	Flat Chest Press	3 x 12-15
	DB Lateral Raise	4 x 15
	Dips (assisted if needed)	2 x 15-20

Week 1, Day 3 – Pulling Strength and Postural Support

This session targets the muscles that stabilize your upper back and shoulders, critical for maintaining posture at full draw. By focusing on pulling movements and high reps, we're developing the muscular endurance needed to keep your scapula engaged and posture upright deep into long training sessions or tournaments. This isn't about max strength but consistent, repeatable form under pressure.

Notes	Exercise	Sets/Reps
	Week 1, Day 3	
	Lat Pulldown	4 x 12
	Chest Supported Row or Cable Row (Neutral Grip, Lat Focused)	4 x 12
	Alternate Row - Pronated Grip - Wide - Upper Back/Rear Delt	3 x 15
	Straight Arm DB Pull Over	3 x 12
	DB Bicep Curl	3 x 15
	DB Hammer Curl	2 x 15

Week 2, Day 1 – Full Body with Increased Volume

Now that your body is adjusting, we're ramping up the volume. This workout reinforces total-body coordination while challenging your muscular endurance further. Every rep should feel intentional. This is where you start to notice the benefits in your shooting, more stability, less shaking, and better recovery between arrows.

Notes	Exercise	Sets/Reps
	Week 2 - Day 1 - Full Body	
	Lying Hamstring Curl	3 x 12-15
	Squat, Leg Press, Hack Squat or Smith Squat	3 x 12-15
	Hip Thrust	2 x 20
	Horizontal Push - Flat Machine Chest Press, BB or DB	3 x 12-15
	Horizontal Pull - Chest Supported Row Machine or Cable Row, BB or DB	3 x 12-15
	Vertical Push - Machine Shoulder Press	2 x 15-20
	Vertical Pull - Lat Pulldown	2 x 15-20

Week 2, Day 2 – Chest and Arms Volume for Draw Control

Today's session builds pressing and pulling endurance in the muscles that help support your draw cycle. You'll hit chest, biceps, and triceps from multiple angles with high reps to encourage blood flow, volume, and fatigue resistance. These muscles stabilize and finesse your shot execution.

Notes	Exercise	Sets/Reps
	Week 2 - Day 2 - Chest/Arms	
Primer	Pec Dec Fly	2 x 12
	Incline Press Machine	3 x 12-15
	Flat Press Machine	3 x 12-15
	Cable or DB Fly	2 x 15
	Machine Preacher Curl	2 x 20
	Machine Tricep Ext	2 x 20
	DB Incline Curl	2 x 15
	DB Overhead Tricep Ext	2 x 15
	Hammer Curl	2 x 15

Week 2, Day 3 – Legs for Power and Endurance

Your legs are your base; they stabilize every shot and absorb fatigue before it reaches your core and shoulders. This lower-body-focused session builds a strong, balanced foundation with extended time under tension. The primer sets activate your muscles, and the supersets and RDLs extend your capacity to stay grounded and balanced.

Notes	Exercise	Sets/Reps
	Week 2 - Day 3 - Legs	
Primer	Hamstring Curl	1 x 15-20
Primer	Leg Extension	1 x 15-20
Primer	Abduction	1 x 15-20
Primer	Adduction	1 x 15-20
	Leg Press, Hack Squat, or Smith Squat	3 x 15-20
	Hip Thrust	3 x 15
	Lying Ham Curl	3 x 12-14
	Leg Extension	3 x 12-14
	RDL	2 x 15
Superset	Abduction	3 x 15-20
	Adduction	3 x 15-20
	Standing Calf	3 x 15-20

Week 3, Day 1 – Full Body Superset Circuit

You've built your base; now, we add density with supersets. This circuit-style full-body workout targets opposing muscle groups to keep your heart rate up and recovery quick. Archery isn't a sprint; it's a marathon. This session teaches your body how to stay composed while fatigued. Maintain good form and breathe with intention as you move from one exercise to the next.

Notes	Exercise	Sets/Reps
	Week 3 - Day 1 - Full Body	
Superset	Lying Hamstring Curl	2 x 20
	Leg Extension	2 x 20
	Squat, Leg Press, Hack Squat or Smith Squat	3 x 20
	Hip Thrust	2 x 20
Superset	Horizontal Push - Flat Machine Chest Press, BB or DB	3 x 15-20
	Horizontal Pull - Chest Supported Row Machine or Cable Row, BB or DB	3 x 15-20
Superset	Vertical Push - Machine Shoulder Press	2 x 15-20
	Vertical Pull - Lat Pulldown	2 x 15-20

Week 3, Day 2 – Chest and Back Supersets for Balanced Upper Body Control

Balanced development between front and back is key for archers. This upper body superset workout will build stamina and symmetry, targeting pushing and pulling muscles with equal volume. Your pecs, lats, delts, and arms all get a complete endurance challenge. It's a smart way to improve posture, shooting mechanics, long-term joint integrity, and overall injury prevention.

Notes	Exercise	Sets/Reps
	Week 3 - Day 2 - Chest/Back	
Superset	Pec Dec Fly	2 x 15
	Rear Delt Fly	2 x 15
Superset	Machine Flat Chest Press	3 x 15-20
	Machine Horizontal Row	3 x 15-20
Superset	Incline Chest Press Machine	3 x 20
	Pronated Lat Pull-Down	3 x 20
Superset	Dips (assisted if needed)	2x 12-15
	Neutral Pull Up (assisted if needed)	2x 12-15
Superset	DB Chest Fly	2 x 15-20
	DB PullOver	2 x 15-20

Week 3, Day 3 – Leg Focus with Supersets and Giant Sets

This is your most demanding leg day yet, designed to simulate the muscular demands of standing, walking challenging terrain on 3D or field courses, or holding positions for hours. Supersets and giant sets will build strength endurance, support joint function, and train your legs to recover faster between ends. Stay focused on form, particularly during RDLs and lunges. Strong legs equal more stable shots and fewer breakdowns under fatigue.

Notes	Exercise	Sets/Reps
	Week 3 - Day 3 - Legs	
Primer	Hamstring Curl	1 x 15-20
Primer	Leg Extension	1 x 15-20
Primer	Abduction	1 x 15-20
Primer	Adduction	1 x 15-20
	Leg Press, Hack Squat, or Smith Squat	3 x 20
Superset	Hip Thrust	2 x 20
	RDL	2 x 20
Superset	Lying Ham Curl	3 x 20
	Leg Extension	3 x 20
Giant Set	Walking Lunges	2 x 15 each
	Abduction	3 x 12-15
	Adduction	3 x 12-15
	Standing Calf Raises	3 x 12

Intermediate 4-day Muscular Endurance Plan

Week 1 – Day 1: Full Body Foundation

This full-body session kicks off your intermediate muscular endurance plan with high-effort, moderate-rep movements designed to push you. By integrating both upper and lower body compound lifts, we're developing total-body fatigue resistance. Focus on smooth, controlled movements and use the rep drops (20–15–12) to progressively increase load while maintaining control.

Notes	Exercise	Sets/Reps
	Week 1, Day 1	
	Lying Hamstring Curl	3 x 10,8,6
	Squat, Leg Press, Hack Squat or Smith Squat	3 x 5-7
	Hip Thrust	2 x 10
	Push - Flat Machine Chest Press, BB or DB	3 x 10,8,6
	Pull - Chest Supported Row Machine or Cable Row, BB or DB	3 x 10,8,6
	Vertical Push - Machine Shoulder Press	2 x 8-10
	Vertical Pull - Lat Pulldown	2 x 8-10

Week 1 – Day 2: Push Power & Precision

Today's focus is all about pushing strength, from shoulders to chest to triceps. These muscle groups are essential for stability at full draw. By targeting them with moderate reps and tempo work, we're improving your ability to stabilize through shot execution. Emphasize time under tension and feel each rep.

Notes	Exercise	Sets/Reps
	Week 1 - Day 2 - Push	
	Shoulder Press	4 x 6
	Flat Chest Press	4 x 6
	Chest Fly Machine	3 x 10
	Lateral Raise	4 x 10
	Tricep Ext	3 x 8
	Push Up or Dip (assisted if needed)	2 x 10-12

Week 1 – Day 3: Back & Biceps – Posture Builders

This workout focuses on pulling movements that reinforce upright posture, scapular control, and the upper back strength critical for archers. These exercises help you stay upright and strong during every shot.

Notes	Exercise	Sets/Reps
	Week 1, Day 3	
	Lat Pulldown	4 x 6
	Chest Supported Row or Cable Row (Neutral Grip, Lat Focused)	4 x 6
	Alternate Row - Pronated Grip - Wide - Upper Back/Rear Delt	3 x 8
	Straight Arm Pull Over	3 x 10
	Preacher Curl Machine	3 x 8
	Hammer Curl	2 x 10

Week 1 – Day 4: Leg Endurance & Control

Lower body stability is your foundation in archery. This session focuses on building strength and muscular endurance in your quads, hamstrings, and glutes, muscles that keep your platform strong and reduce sway over long competitions. Our stability starts from the ground up.

Notes	Exercise	Sets/Reps
	Week 1 - Day 4 - Legs	
	Leg Press, Hack Squat, Smith Squat, or Squat	4 x 8-10
	Hip Thrust	3 x 10
	45 Degree Hip Extension	2 x 10
	Hamstring Curl	3 x 8
	Leg Extension	3 x 8
Superset	Hip Abduction	2 x 10
	Hip Adduction	2 x 10
	Standing Calf	4 x 8

Week 2 – Day 1: Full Body Conditioning

We're back to a full-body format to reinforce strength across all movement patterns. These moderate-rep sets push your aerobic endurance while continuing to build postural integrity. Treat each movement as a skill session. Clean mechanics under fatigue will carry over into higher-quality practice sessions and better shot consistency.

Notes	Exercise	Sets/Reps
	Week 2 - Day 1 - Full Body	
	Lying Hamstring Curl	3 x 10-12
	Squat, Leg Press, Hack Squat or Smith Squat	3 x 8-12
	Hip Thrust	2 x 12
	Horizontal Push - Flat Machine Chest Press, BB or DB	3 x 8-12
	Horizontal Pull - Chest Supported Row Machine or Cable Row, BB or DB	3 x 8-12
	Vertical Push - Machine Shoulder Press	2 x 10-12
	Vertical Pull - Lat Pulldown	2 x 10-12

Week 2 – Day 2: Chest & Arms – Shot Stability Focus

Today's session targets your chest, triceps, and biceps in a volume format to build resilience and endurance in your shot-stabilizing muscles. Work for high-quality reps, stay controlled, and avoid locking out or rushing between movements.

Notes	Exercise	Sets/Reps
	Week 2 - Day 2 - Chest/Arms	
Primer	Pec Dec Fly	2 x 10
	Incline Press Machine	3 x 8-12
	Flat Press Machine	3 x 8-12
	Cable or DB Fly	2 x 10
	Machine Preacher Curl	2 x 12
	Machine Tricep Ext	2 x 12
	DB Incline Curl	2 x 12
	DB Overhead Tricep Ext	2 x 12
	Hammer Curl	2 x 10

Week 2 – Day 3: Back & Shoulders – Anchor & Hold

Today's focus is all about your ability to hold and finish a shot with strength. These pulling and pressing exercises reinforce scapular control, shoulder health, and rear delt endurance.

Notes	Exercise	Sets/Reps
	Week 2 - Day 3 - Back/Shoulders	
Primer	Straight Arm Pulldown	2 x 10
	Shoulder Press Machine	3 x 8-12
	Lat Pulldown	3 x 8-12
	Upper Back Row - Pronated Wide	3 x 8-12
	Cable Row - Lat Focused	3 x 8-12
	Lateral Raise	3 x 10-15
	Upright Row	3 x 15
	Rear Delt Fly	2 x 15

Week 2 – Day 4: Legs – Long Hold Foundation

This lower-body session leans into endurance and symmetry. You'll train with higher volume and targeted isolation to build single-leg control, reduce imbalances, and increase fatigue resistance. These qualities are essential for long days on uneven terrain or standing still through long days.

Notes	Exercise	Sets/Reps
	Week 2 - Day 4 - Legs	
Primer	Hamstring Curl	1 x 15-20
Primer	Leg Extension	1 x 15-20
Primer	Abduction	1 x 15-20
Primer	Adduction	1 x 15-20
	Leg Press, Hack Squat, or Smith Squat	3 x 12
	Hip Thrust	3 x 15
	Lying Ham Curl	3 x 12-14
	Leg Extension	3 x 12-14
	RDL	2 x 15
Superset	Abduction	3 x 12-15
	Adduction	3 x 12-15
	Standing Calf	3 x 12

Week 3 – Day 1: Superset Full Body Endurance

Supersets today mean minimal rest, maximum output. This full-body session teaches you to stay composed under muscular fatigue, perfect training for the mental grind of long tournaments. Push yourself to move and keep reps controlled even when you're tired. This is where mental toughness and physical preparation meet.

Notes	Exercise	Sets/Reps
	Week 3 - Day 1 - Full Body	
Superset	Lying Hamstring Curl	2 x 20
	Leg Extension	2 x 20
	Squat, Leg Press, Hack Squat or Smith Squat	3 x 20
	Hip Thrust	2 x 20
Superset	Horizontal Push - Flat Machine Chest Press, BB or DB	3 x 15-20
	Horizontal Pull - Chest Supported Row Machine or Cable Row, BB or DB	3 x 15-20
Superset	Vertical Push - Machine Shoulder Press	2 x 15-20
	Vertical Pull - Lat Pulldown	2 x 15-20

Week 3 – Day 2: Chest & Back – Oppositional Strength

Chest and back are antagonists in movement, but allies in posture and control. This superset-focused day helps you develop equal pulling and pushing strength. For archery, this translates to greater balance between the bow side and draw side. Prioritize full range of motion and controlled negatives on each rep.

Notes	Exercise	Sets/Reps
	Week 3 - Day 2 - Chest/Back	
Superset	Pec Dec Fly	2 x 15
	Rear Delt Fly	2 x 15
Superset	Machine Flat Chest Press	3 x 15-20
	Machine Horizontal Row	3 x 15-20
Superset	Incline Chest Press Machine	3 x 20
	Pronated Lat Pull-Down	3 x 20
Superset	Dips (assisted if needed)	2x 12-15
	Neutral Pull Up (assisted if needed)	2x 12-15
Superset	DB Chest Fly	2 x 15-20
	DB PullOver	2 x 15-20

Week 3 – Day 3: Shoulders & Arms – Finish with Strength

This is your pump day, but with a purpose. Strong shoulders and arms mean stable shots, reduced fatigue, and better bow control. Use these supersets and giant sets to challenge yourself to maintain good form even as the burn kicks in. Time under tension here equals time under control on the shooting line.

Notes	Exercise	Sets/Reps
	Week 3 - Day 3 - Shoulders/Arms	
	Machine Lateral Raise	2 x 20
	Machine Shoulder Press	2 x 20
Giant Set	DB Lateral Raise	2 x 12
	DB Front Raise	2 x 12
	DB Rear Delt Fly	2 x 12
Superset	DB Arnold Press	2 x 15
	DB Upright Row	2 x 15
Superset	DB Spider Curl	2 x 15
	DB Tricep Kickback	2 x 15
Superset	Preacher Curl	2 x 15
	Machine Tricep Ext	2 x 15
Superset	DB Incline Curl	2 x 15
	DB Overhead Ext	2 x 15

Week 3 – Day 4: Legs – Endurance Grind

This is a leg day to remember. Long sets, supersets, and giant sets combine to create deep fatigue and unmatched muscular endurance. This translates directly to your ability to stay strong and steady through tournaments and long days of training. Focus on breath, form, and finishing every rep with intention.

Notes	Exercise	Sets/Reps
	Week 3 - Day 4 - Legs	
Primer	Hamstring Curl	1 x 15-20
Primer	Leg Extension	1 x 15-20
Primer	Abduction	1 x 15-20
Primer	Adduction	1 x 15-20
	Leg Press, Hack Squat, or Smith Squat	3 x 20
Superset	Hip Thrust	2 x 20
	RDL	2 x 20
Superset	Lying Ham Curl	3 x 20
	Leg Extension	3 x 20
Giant Set	Walking Lunges	2 x 15 each
	Abduction	3 x 12-15
	Adduction	3 x 12-15
	Standing Calf Raises	3 x 12

Advanced 5-Day Muscular Endurance Plan

Day 1 – Upper Body Strength & Density

Welcome to Day 1 of the Advanced Muscular Endurance program, where we launch into a high-volume upper body session that targets every major muscle group across the chest, back, shoulders, and arms. This workout is built for experienced archers ready to handle serious muscular endurance demands while still chasing hypertrophy and definition. Expect to alternate between presses and rows, with an emphasis on movement control and full range of motion. By layering in push-pull supersets and finishing with focused arm work, this session builds balanced upper body strength to support better bow stability and endurance in long shooting sessions.

Notes	Exercise	Sets/Reps
	Hypertrophy Advanced - Day 1 - Upper	
	DB Chest Press	3 x 15-20
	Chest Supported DB Row	3 x 12-15
	HS Incline Press	3 x 12
	HS Incline Row	3 x 10-12
	Barbell Decline Press	3 x 12-15
	Cable Low Row	3 x 15
	Chest Supported DB Lateral Raise	3 x 15-20
	DB Skull Crushers	3x 10-12
	DB Preacher Curl	3 x 10-12

Day 2 – Posterior Chain & Lower Body Power

Day 2 zeroes in on your lower half with a serious posterior chain focus. From high-rep leg curls to heavy squats and Romanian deadlifts, this session trains your glutes, hamstrings, and quads to generate power, stability, and resilience under fatigue. We're training for stamina as much as strength, using higher reps to push through the burn and build legs that won't quit, whether you're climbing rugged terrain on a 3D course or standing strong for scoring arrow number 72. Keep rest minimal and as always, prioritize proper movement over load.

Notes	Exercise	Sets/Reps
	Hypertrophy Advanced - Day 2 - Lower	
	Lying Leg Curl	3 x 20,15,12
	Barbell Squat	4 x 10
	Glute Bridge	3 x 12-15
	Romanian Deadlift	3 x 15-20
	Leg Extension Machine	3 x 15-20
	Standing Calf Raise	4 x 15-20
	Machine Abduction	2x 20
	Machine Adduction	2x 20

Day 3 – Push Volume & Shoulder Resilience

Today's push day turns up the volume with layered press variations and high-rep triceps work. This workout strengthens your entire anterior chain, chest, shoulders, and triceps, while reinforcing posture and control for shooting your best. The blend of dumbbell, barbell, machine, and bodyweight exercises will torch your pushing muscles while training them for long-lasting output. Prioritize time under tension and slow and controlled reps. This is the kind of muscular endurance work that translates directly to a steadier shot and a more repeatable and consistent process over time.

Notes	Exercise	Sets/Reps
	Hypertrophy Advanced - Day 3 - Push	
	Incline Barbell Press	4 x 12
	DB Chest Press	3 x 15
	DB Overhead Press	3 x 12-15
	Machine or DB Lateral Raise	3 x 20
	Incline DB Fly (Low to High)	3 x 12-15
	Cable Fly	3 x 10-12
	Rope Tri Extensions	3x 15-20
	DB Skull Crushers	3x 10-12
	Tricep Pushups	3 x 12-15

Day 4 – Pulling Power & Grip Control

Your fourth session attacks the back and biceps. Pull-ups, rows, and deadlifts build dense, functional pulling strength that supports scapular control and posture, keys to keeping your bow arm stable and strong through the shot. The added volume on lats, traps, and grip muscles ensures you're developing the kind of back strength archery athletes need to maintain tension and form throughout long tournaments.

Notes	Exercise	Sets/Reps
	Hypertrophy Advanced - Day 4 - Pull	
	Cable Pull In	2 x 15
	Pull-up (assisted if needed)	3 x RPE 9
	Chest Supported DB Row	3 x 12-15
	HS High Row	3 x 10-15
	HS Low Row	3 x 10-15
	Deadlift	3 x 12-15
	DB Pullover	2 x 15-20
	Incline DB Curl	3 x 15-20
	Hammer Curl	2 x 15

Day 5 – Lower Body Volume & Isolation

We close the week with another intense lower-body day, but this time with more isolation and volume-based finishers. This leg day hammers your adductors, glutes, quads, hamstrings, and calves using a strategic mix of compound and single-leg movements. It's perfect for dialing in symmetry, stability, and joint control, essential for archers who need to remain steady during windy conditions. Expect fatigue and a huge pump. Finish strong, and use this day to polish your strength and resilience from the ground up.

Notes	Exercise	Sets/Reps
	Hypertrophy Advanced - Day 5 - Lower	
	Machine Adduction	3 x 20
	Machine Abduction	3 x 20
	Barbell Squat	3 x 12-15
	Leg Extensions	3 x 15-20
	DB Bulgarian Split Squat	3 x 12 (each leg)
	Leg Press	2x 20
	Seated or Lying Leg Curl	2x 20
	Calf Raises	3 x 20

CHAPTER 8

HYPERTROPHY FOR ARCHERY

O f all the training styles available to archers, hypertrophy strikes a unique and beneficial balance. It builds muscle size and strength, boosts muscular endurance, and, thanks to its shorter rest periods, elevates cardiovascular demand. This makes it an ideal training method for archers seeking a complete, efficient workout that supports both physical performance and mental resilience. Hypertrophy training conditions the body to handle repeated muscular effort under fatigue, reinforcing the stability needed for shot consistency while fostering the kind of control and discipline that sharpens the mind. It's a method that demands focus through discomfort and teaches the body to recover quickly both skills that translate directly to competition.

The hypertrophy workouts in this chapter are designed to support archery performance through full-body strength training.

Based upon your current training level and the amount of time you can devote to exercise, there are beginner 3-day, intermediate 4-day, and advanced 5-day per week programs to elevate your archery performance, body and mind.

Beginner 3-Day Hypertrophy Plan

Week 1 – Day 1: Full Body Strength Foundation

Welcome to your first hypertrophy workout! This session sets the tone by targeting major movement patterns across your whole body, hinge, squat, push, and pull. You'll work through compound lifts like squats and rows to build a strong foundation, while isolation movements like hamstring curls and lat pulldowns add focused volume. Today's lower rep ranges allow you to explore strength within hypertrophy training. Move with control, emphasize time under tension, and focus on perfecting the movement over heavy weight. In the same way we don't want to sacrifice archery form for a higher draw weight. This is about teaching your muscles how to work efficiently while preparing your joints, tendons, and nervous system for what's ahead.

Notes	Exercise	Sets/Reps
	Week 1, Day 1	
	Lying Hamstring Curl	3 x 10,8,6
	Squat, Leg Press, Hack Squat or Smith Squat	3 x 5-7
	Hip Thrust	2 x 10
	Push - Flat Machine Chest Press, BB or DB	3 x 10,8,6
	Pull - Chest Supported Row Machine or Cable Row, BB or DB	3 x 10,8,6
	Vertical Push - Machine Shoulder Press	2 x 8-10
	Vertical Pull - Lat Pulldown	2 x 8-10

Week 1 – Day 2: Athletic Strength and Shoulder Stability

This workout hits the legs, shoulders, and chest with a balance of unilateral and bilateral movements. Walking lunges challenge coordination, balance, and control, while pressing movements build upper body mass and shoulder endurance, all key areas for archers. Dips and lateral raises finish off your arms and delts with intensity. Take your time with each rep, control the tempo, and don't rush through the finish. Movement quality is still your top priority.

Notes	Exercise	Sets/Reps
	Week 1 - Day 2	
	DB Walking Lunges	3 x 8
	DB Shoulder Press	3 x 10
	Lying Hamstring Curl	3 x 10
	Flat Chest Press	3 x 10
	DB Lateral Raise	4 x 10
	Dips (assisted if needed)	2 x 10-12

Week 1 – Day 3: Back and Arms Focus

Today is all about pulling strength, upper back development, and arm hypertrophy. A strong back and stable shoulders are critical for an archer's control. We're targeting all angles of the lats, upper traps, and rear delts, finishing with focused bicep work. Stick to strict form, in other words, don't swing your body or use momentum through the rows or curls. Feel every rep, use a weight that lets you control the negative, and think stretch and squeeze.

Notes	Exercise	Sets/Reps
	Week 1, Day 3	
	Lat Pulldown	4 x 6
	Chest Supported Row or Cable Row (Neutral Grip, Lat Focused)	4 x 6
	Alternate Row - Pronated Grip - Wide - Upper Back/Rear Delt	3 x 8
	Straight Arm DB Pull Over	3 x 10
	DB Bicep Curl	3 x 8
	DB Hammer Curl	2 x 10

Week 2 – Day 1: Full Body Volume with Control

This week, we're turning up the volume with slightly higher rep ranges and more time under tension. This full-body session keeps the same core movement patterns but with a hypertrophy-focused rep scheme (8–12). Push yourself, but only as far as you can maintain good form and control. Every exercise should feel purposeful. Archery requires strength that lasts over time and today builds that kind of capacity.

Notes	Exercise	Sets/Reps
	Week 2 - Day 1 - Full Body	
	Lying Hamstring Curl	3 x 10-12
	Squat, Leg Press, Hack Squat or Smith Squat	3 x 8-12
	Hip Thrust	2 x 12
	Horizontal Push - Flat Machine Chest Press, BB or DB	3 x 8-12
	Horizontal Pull - Chest Supported Row Machine or Cable Row, BB or DB	3 x 8-12
	Vertical Push - Machine Shoulder Press	2 x 10-12
	Vertical Pull - Lat Pulldown	2 x 10-12

Week 2 – Day 2: Chest & Arms Hypertrophy

Today is a classic upper-body day with a modern hypertrophy twist. You'll start by opening the chest and mind-muscle connection with fly movements, then press heavy and finish with focused isolation on biceps and triceps. These are your volume builders. Archers benefit from strong, stable shoulders and arms that can handle repetitive stress; this is where that durability begins. Use slow, controlled reps, and pause where you feel the muscle working hardest.

Notes	Exercise	Sets/Reps
	Week 2 - Day 2 - Chest/Arms	
Primer	Pec Dec Fly	2 x 10
	Incline Press Machine	3 x 8-12
	Flat Press Machine	3 x 8-12
	Cable or DB Fly	2 x 10
	Machine Preacher Curl	2 x 12
	Machine Tricep Ext	2 x 12
	DB Incline Curl	2 x 12
	DB Overhead Tricep Ext	2 x 12
	Hammer Curl	2 x 10

Week 2 – Day 3: Posterior Chain & Leg Power

Leg day gets serious. From priming movements to targeted glutes, hamstrings, and quads, this session builds the base every archer needs for stability on the line. Expect to feel the burn, but also expect to feel stronger afterward. Supersets and higher reps target endurance, mobility, and strength in the hips and legs. Remember: the ground is your foundation.

Notes	Exercise	Sets/Reps
	Week 2 - Day 3 - Legs	
Primer	Hamstring Curl	1 x 15-20
Primer	Leg Extension	1 x 15-20
Primer	Abduction	1 x 15-20
Primer	Adduction	1 x 15-20
	Leg Press, Hack Squat, or Smith Squat	3 x 12
	Hip Thrust	3 x 15
	Lying Ham Curl	3 x 12-14
	Leg Extension	3 x 12-14
	RDL	2 x 15
Superset	Abduction	3 x 12-15
	Adduction	3 x 12-15
	Standing Calf	3 x 12

Week 3 – Day 1: Full Body Giant Volume

This week, we push volume to the max. Long sets, supersets, and a full-body workload challenge your muscular endurance and mental grit. With sets of 15–20 reps, your focus is on consistency and control. This type of work builds not just muscle, but the focus and breathing control essential for high-performance archery. This is as much a mental workout as it is physical.

Notes	Exercise	Sets/Reps
	Week 3 - Day 1 - Full Body	
Superset	Lying Hamstring Curl	2 x 20
	Leg Extension	2 x 20
	Squat, Leg Press, Hack Squat or Smith Squat	3 x 20
	Hip Thrust	2 x 20
Superset	Horizontal Push - Flat Machine Chest Press, BB or DB	3 x 15-20
	Horizontal Pull - Chest Supported Row Machine or Cable Row, BB or DB	3 x 15-20
Superset	Vertical Push - Machine Shoulder Press	2 x 15-20
	Vertical Pull - Lat Pulldown	2 x 15-20

Week 3 – Day 2: Chest & Back Superset Smash

Today is built around supersets, pairing opposing muscle groups to maximize time efficiency and pump. Chest and back work together to support scapular control, posture, and draw strength. These large muscle groups also regulate much of your physical output, so training them well supports long-term performance. Use moderate loads, keep the rest short (60-90s), and emphasize the stretch and contraction on each movement.

Notes	Exercise	Sets/Reps
	Week 3 - Day 2 - Chest/Back	
Superset	Pec Dec Fly	2 x 15
	Rear Delt Fly	2 x 15
Superset	Machine Flat Chest Press	3 x 15-20
	Machine Horizontal Row	3 x 15-20
Superset	Incline Chest Press Machine	3 x 20
	Pronated Lat Pull-Down	3 x 20
Superset	Dips (assisted if needed)	2x 12-15
	Neutral Pull Up (assisted if needed)	2x 12-15
Superset	DB Chest Fly	2 x 15-20
	DB PullOver	2 x 15-20

Week 3 – Day 3: Legs and Glutes – Stamina Meets Strength

Leg day closes the week with high reps, supersets, and a giant set finisher that will leave your glutes and thighs burning. You'll start with activation primers, then move into deep work on every major leg muscle group. This session mimics the sustained effort needed during long training days or competition, reinforcing the mental focus needed to stay strong through the final ends. Don't rush. Each rep should feel like it has a purpose.

Notes	Exercise	Sets/Reps
	Week 3 - Day 3 - Legs	
Primer	Hamstring Curl	1 x 15-20
Primer	Leg Extension	1 x 15-20
Primer	Abduction	1 x 15-20
Primer	Adduction	1 x 15-20
	Leg Press, Hack Squat, or Smith Squat	3 x 20
Superset	Hip Thrust	2 x 20
	RDL	2 x 20
Superset	Lying Ham Curl	3 x 20
	Leg Extension	3 x 20
Giant Set	Walking Lunges	2 x 15 each
	Abduction	3 x 12-15
	Adduction	3 x 12-15
	Standing Calf Raises	3 x 12

Intermediate 4-day Hypertrophy Plan

Week 1 – Day 1: Full Body Foundation

Welcome to the start of your intermediate hypertrophy program! Today's full-body workout sets the tone for the week by targeting every major muscle group with purpose and precision. We begin with posterior chain work to build power and stability in the hamstrings and glutes. Moving into compound lifts like squats and presses, we emphasize strength through lower rep ranges, encouraging controlled movement and heavier loads while still prioritizing form. Each push and pull exercise is strategically placed to improve muscular balance and promote symmetry. Time under tension will be key, don't rush the reps. Focus on clean, intentional movement. This is your chance to develop a body that supports high-level performance shot after shot.

Notes	Exercise	Sets/Reps
	Week 1, Day 1	
	Lying Hamstring Curl	3 x 10,8,6
	Squat, Leg Press, Hack Squat or Smith Squat	3 x 5-7
	Hip Thrust	2 x 10
	Push - Flat Machine Chest Press, BB or DB	3 x 10,8,6
	Pull - Chest Supported Row Machine or Cable Row, BB or DB	3 x 10,8,6
	Vertical Push - Machine Shoulder Press	2 x 8-10
	Vertical Pull - Lat Pulldown	2 x 8-10

Week 1 – Day 2: Push Strength

Today is all about upper body pushing power with the chest, shoulders, and triceps. This session is designed to increase strength and muscle density through pressing variations. The shoulder press and chest press take center stage with lower rep ranges to stimulate growth through mechanical tension. You'll finish with accessory work like lateral raises and triceps extensions to isolate and sculpt. As always, prioritize range of motion and control, especially on the eccentric (lowering) phase.

Notes	Exercise	Sets/Reps
	Week 1 - Day 2 - Push	
	Shoulder Press	4 x 6
	Flat Chest Press	4 x 6
	Chest Fly Machine	3 x 10
	Lateral Raise	4 x 10
	Tricep Ext	3 x 8
	Push Up or Dip (assisted if needed)	2 x 10-12

Week 1 – Day 3: Pull and Posture

A strong back isn't just for aesthetics, it's essential for archery power, stability, and postural integrity. Today's pull session zeroes in on your lats, traps, rhomboids, and biceps. Each movement is selected to enhance your ability to control the bow, stabilize through the shot, and resist fatigue during long days. Rows and pull-downs take priority, and grip variation ensures we hit every angle of your back. You'll wrap up with curls to build arm endurance and strength. Focus on tempo, squeezing the muscles at peak contraction, and controlling the negative.

Notes	Exercise	Sets/Reps
	Week 1, Day 3	
	Lat Pulldown	4 x 6
	Chest Supported Row or Cable Row (Neutral Grip, Lat Focused)	4 x 6
	Alternate Row - Pronated Grip - Wide - Upper Back/Rear Delt	3 x 8
	Straight Arm Pull Over	3 x 10
	Preacher Curl Machine	3 x 8
	Hammer Curl	2 x 10

Week 1 – Day 4: Leg Power and Core Control

Lower body strength fuels upper body stability. Today we're pushing your legs and hips to build a solid foundation for everything above the waist. Squats and leg presses give you the horsepower, while hip thrusts and hamstring curls develop the posterior chain, supporting an archer's stability. Finish with hip abduction/adduction work and calf raises to round out the lower body.

Notes	Exercise	Sets/Reps
	Week 1 - Day 4 - Legs	
	Leg Press, Hack Squat, Smith Squat, or Squat	4 x 8-10
	Hip Thrust	3 x 10
	45 Degree Hip Extension	2 x 10
	Hamstring Curl	3 x 8
	Leg Extension	3 x 8
Superset	Hip Abduction	2 x 10
	Hip Adduction	2 x 10
	Standing Calf	4 x 8

Week 2 – Day 1: Total Body Volume

You're back to a full-body focus, but with a volume progression. This workout blends strength and hypertrophy ranges to challenge muscle endurance while maintaining movement quality. You'll revisit major lifts from Week 1, but this time with slightly higher reps and emphasis on consistent tension. Think of this as your reinforcement day. Every lift contributes to postural control, shot stability, and long-term joint health. Time under tension is your ally; maximize the work each muscle does per set.

Notes	Exercise	Sets/Reps
	Week 2 - Day 1 - Full Body	
	Lying Hamstring Curl	3 x 10-12
	Squat, Leg Press, Hack Squat or Smith Squat	3 x 8-12
	Hip Thrust	2 x 12
	Horizontal Push - Flat Machine Chest Press, BB or DB	3 x 8-12
	Horizontal Pull - Chest Supported Row Machine or Cable Row, BB or DB	3 x 8-12
	Vertical Push - Machine Shoulder Press	2 x 10-12
	Vertical Pull - Lat Pulldown	2 x 10-12

Week 2 – Day 2: Chest and Arms Isolation

Today is for building pressing power and arm endurance. Starting with a chest fly primer activates the pecs before you hit compound pressing movements. Then, it's all about fine-tuning the details with isolation work for biceps and triceps. The goal is to pump volume into these supporting muscles, reinforcing muscular endurance and resilience under load. Move through each rep with control, especially during eccentrics.

Notes	Exercise	Sets/Reps
	Week 2 - Day 2 - Chest/Arms	
Primer	Pec Dec Fly	2 x 10
	Incline Press Machine	3 x 8-12
	Flat Press Machine	3 x 8-12
	Cable or DB Fly	2 x 10
	Machine Preacher Curl	2 x 12
	Machine Tricep Ext	2 x 12
	DB Incline Curl	2 x 12
	DB Overhead Tricep Ext	2 x 12
	Hammer Curl	2 x 10

Week 2 – Day 3: Back and Shoulders Balance

Balance is key in both your physique and your shot. This workout hones in on posterior chain and deltoid development, providing structural support for your archery technique. Supersets and primers help you pre-activate the right muscles so you feel each rep where you're supposed to. You'll mix vertical and horizontal pulls, wide and neutral grips, and add rear delt work to reinforce scapular control and shoulder health. Shoulder burnout finishers build muscular endurance where it matters most for a steady aim.

Notes	Exercise	Sets/Reps
	Week 2 - Day 3 - Back/Shoulders	
Primer	Straight Arm Pulldown	2 x 10
	Shoulder Press Machine	3 x 8-12
	Lat Pulldown	3 x 8-12
	Upper Back Row - Pronated Wide	3 x 8-12
	Cable Row - Lat Focused	3 x 8-12
	Lateral Raise	3 x 10-15
	Upright Row	3 x 15
	Rear Delt Fly	2 x 15

Week 2 – Day 4: Leg Day – Endurance and Range

This lower body session blends strength, mobility, and hypertrophy into one powerful sequence. After primer sets to activate every muscle group around your hips, you'll move into a structured progression targeting quads, hamstrings, glutes, and calves. Reps climb higher here, increasing endurance and promoting blood flow, an essential step for recovery and muscular adaptation. Supersets keep intensity high while maintaining time under tension. Be deliberate with every eccentric and don't cheat the depth.

Notes	Exercise	Sets/Reps
	Week 2 - Day 4 - Legs	
Primer	Hamstring Curl	1 x 15-20
Primer	Leg Extension	1 x 15-20
Primer	Abduction	1 x 15-20
Primer	Adduction	1 x 15-20
	Leg Press, Hack Squat, or Smith Squat	3 x 12
	Hip Thrust	3 x 15
	Lying Ham Curl	3 x 12-14
	Leg Extension	3 x 12-14
	RDL	2 x 15
Superset	Abduction	3 x 12-15
	Adduction	3 x 12-15
	Standing Calf	3 x 12

Week 3 – Day 1: Full Body Burnout

Welcome to Week 3, a high-volume full-body challenge designed to push your limits. Today's workout uses supersets to maintain time under tension across all major movement patterns. Lighter weight with more reps demands control and discipline. This is where you polish your form and build the mental grit needed for long competition days. Supersetting opposing movement patterns (push/pull, extension/flexion) will amplify your conditioning while still focusing on hypertrophy.

Notes	Exercise	Sets/Reps
	Week 3 - Day 1 - Full Body	
Superset	Lying Hamstring Curl	2 x 20
	Leg Extension	2 x 20
	Squat, Leg Press, Hack Squat or Smith Squat	3 x 20
	Hip Thrust	2 x 20
Superset	Horizontal Push - Flat Machine Chest Press, BB or DB	3 x 15-20
	Horizontal Pull - Chest Supported Row Machine or Cable Row, BB or DB	3 x 15-20
Superset	Vertical Push - Machine Shoulder Press	2 x 15-20
	Vertical Pull - Lat Pulldown	2 x 15-20

Week 3 – Day 2: Chest and Back Superset Smash

Today is all about upper body supersets, pushing and pulling back-to-back to drive blood flow, challenge muscular endurance, and accelerate hypertrophy. This is high-volume work with relatively short rest, so you'll need to manage your breathing and stay focused. Each pair of movements is designed to target complementary areas of the upper body, reinforcing stability and symmetry for archery performance.

Notes	Exercise	Sets/Reps
	Week 3 - Day 2 - Chest/Back	
Superset	Pec Dec Fly	2 x 15
	Rear Delt Fly	2 x 15
Superset	Machine Flat Chest Press	3 x 15-20
	Machine Horizontal Row	3 x 15-20
Superset	Incline Chest Press Machine	3 x 20
	Pronated Lat Pull-Down	3 x 20
Superset	Dips (assisted if needed)	2x 12-15
	Neutral Pull Up (assisted if needed)	2x 12-15
Superset	DB Chest Fly	2 x 15-20
	DB PullOver	2 x 15-20

Week 3 – Day 3: Shoulders and Arms Giant Set

We're dialing in shoulder definition and arm strength with focused isolation work and giant sets. You'll cycle through lateral, front, and rear delt movements, followed by curls and extensions targeting all angles of the arms. Giant sets challenge your muscular endurance while keeping rest short and stimulus high. Control each rep, especially in the lowering phase, and feel the muscle work throughout its entire range. These muscles may be small, but they considerably affect archery stability.

Notes	Exercise	Sets/Reps
	Week 3 - Day 3 - Shoulders/Arms	
	Machine Lateral Raise	2 x 20
	Machine Shoulder Press	2 x 20
Giant Set	DB Lateral Raise	2 x 12
	DB Front Raise	2 x 12
	DB Rear Delt Fly	2 x 12
Superset	DB Arnold Press	2 x 15
	DB Upright Row	2 x 15
Superset	DB Spider Curl	2 x 15
	DB Tricep Kickback	2 x 15
Superset	Preacher Curl	2 x 15
	Machine Tricep Ext	2 x 15
Superset	DB Incline Curl	2 x 15
	DB Overhead Ext	2 x 15

Week 3 – Day 4: Legs – Volume and Symmetry

Your final workout this week is a true leg finisher. You've built the strength, now we're stacking endurance, symmetry, and refined control. Primer sets wake up every muscle around the hips and knees, then you'll dive into high-rep sets with supersets and giant sets to keep intensity sky high. You'll finish with lunges, adductors, abductors, and calves, small movements that create big gains in balance and support. Remember, the stronger and more stable your lower body, the steadier your upper body can be at full draw.

Notes	Exercise	Sets/Reps
	Week 3 - Day 4 - Legs	
Primer	Hamstring Curl	1 x 15-20
Primer	Leg Extension	1 x 15-20
Primer	Abduction	1 x 15-20
Primer	Adduction	1 x 15-20
	Leg Press, Hack Squat, or Smith Squat	3 x 20
Superset	Hip Thrust	2 x 20
	RDL	2 x 20
Superset	Lying Ham Curl	3 x 20
	Leg Extension	3 x 20
Giant Set	Walking Lunges	2 x 15 each
	Abduction	3 x 12-15
	Adduction	3 x 12-15
	Standing Calf Raises	3 x 12

Hypertrophy Advanced 5-Day Plan

Day 1 – Upper Body Strength & Volume

This workout kicks off your week with a powerful upper-body focus designed to stimulate maximum hypertrophy in both pushing and pulling muscles. With exercises targeting the chest, back, and arms, the goal is to build dense, functional muscle mass that supports postural strength and shot stability. Emphasize time under tension during each set, especially during eccentric phases, and prioritize form over the weight being used. As you progress week to week, aim to add a rep or increase the weight to maintain muscle adaptation and challenge.

Notes	Exercise	Sets/Reps
	Hypertrophy Advanced - Day 1 - Upper	
	DB Chest Press	3 x 10-12
	Chest Supported DB Row	3 x 10-12
	HS Incline Press	3 x 8
	HS Incline Row	3 x 8-10
	Barbell Decline Press	3 x 10-12
	Cable Low Row	3 x 10
	Chest Supported DB Lateral Raise	3 x 12-15
	DB Skull Crushers	3x 8-10
	DB Preacher Curl	3 x 8-10

Day 2 – Lower Body Power & Posterior Chain Development

Your foundation as an archer starts from the ground up. Today's session builds strength and size in the glutes, hamstrings, quads, and calves, reinforcing lower body stability and helping you stay grounded through each shot. Movements like barbell squats and RDLs demand strict attention to technique and control, this isn't about chasing heavy numbers, it's about moving well under tension. Stick to full range of motion and drive each rep with purpose. Focus on weekly progression while never sacrificing form.

Notes	Exercise	Sets/Reps
	Hypertrophy Advanced - Day 2 - Lower	
	Lying Leg Curl	3 x 10
	Barbell Squat	4 x 8
	Glute Bridge	3 x 10-12
	Romanian Deadlift	3 x 10-15
	Leg Extension Machine	3 x 10-15
	Standing Calf Raise	4 x 10-15
	Machine Abduction	2x 15-20
	Machine Adduction	2x 15-20

Day 3 – Push: Chest, Shoulders & Triceps Focus

This push-dominant day targets the entire front-side of your upper body, chest, shoulders, and triceps, with a blend of compound lifts and isolation work. These muscles play a vital role in maintaining bow arm position and follow-through stability. Keep your tempo controlled and your movement smooth. Isolation lifts like lateral raises and triceps extensions are perfect for refining the small stabilizers often overlooked. Time under tension is your best friend here, so move intentionally and squeeze every rep.

Notes	Exercise	Sets/Reps
	Hypertrophy Advanced - Day 3 - Push	
	Incline Barbell Press	4 x 8
	DB Chest Press	3 x 10
	DB Overhead Press	3 x 10
	Machine or DB Lateral Raise	3 x 10-15
	Incline DB Fly (Low to High)	3 x 10-12
	Cable Fly	3 x 10-12
	Rope Tri Extensions	3x 12-15
	DB Skull Crushers	3x 6-8
	Tricep Pushups	3 x 10-15

Day 4 – Pull: Back & Biceps Strength for Control and Recovery

A strong back is a strong anchor point. This session is all about building the lats, traps, rhomboids, and biceps, muscles essential for consistent draw control and a stable hold. Compound rows and pull-ups set the foundation, while accessory lifts like curls and DB pullovers round out the hypertrophy work. Focus on scapular retraction and controlled tempo during all pulling movements. Use progressive overload strategies to grow, but never rush through your range, feel the muscle work with every inch.

Notes	Exercise	Sets/Reps
	Hypertrophy Advanced - Day 4 - Pull	
	Cable Pull In	2 x 10
	Pull-up (assisted if needed)	3 x RPE 9
	Chest Supported DB Row	3 x 8-10
	HS High Row	3 x 8-10
	HS Low Row	3 x 8-10
	Deadlift	3 x 8-10
	DB Pullover	2 x 12-15
	Incline DB Curl	3 x 12-15
	Hammer Curl	2 x 10-12

Day 5 – Lower Body Hypertrophy & Unilateral Strength

Finish the week by reinforcing your lower body with a hypertrophy-focused leg day that blends bilateral and unilateral work. Bulgarian split squats, leg presses, and curls target every major muscle group in the lower body while also challenging balance, proprioception, and control, key qualities for archery athletes holding a steady stance under pressure. Use this day to emphasize slower tempos, long eccentric phases, and smooth, clean reps. As fatigue sets in, keep your mental focus sharp and finish the week strong.

Notes	Exercise	Sets/Reps
	Hypertrophy Advanced - Day 5 - Lower	
	Machine Adduction	3 x 12-15
	Machine Abduction	3 x 12-15
	Barbell Squat	3 x 10-12
	Leg Extensions	3 x 10-15
	DB Bulgarian Split Squat	3 x 8 (each leg)
	Leg Press	2x 12-15
	Seated or Lying Leg Curl	2x 12-15
	Calf Raises	3 x 15-20

CHAPTER 9

HIGH-INTENSITY INTERVAL TRAINING (HIIT)

High-Intensity Interval Training, or HIIT, is where physical grit meets mental toughness. These workouts are fast-paced, demanding, and deliberately uncomfortable, making them an ideal tool for archers who want to train not only their bodies but also their minds. HIIT pushes you through cycles of intense effort followed by short recovery periods, developing aerobic capacity, muscular endurance, and strength all at once. But beyond the physical gains, it teaches an archer the mental discipline of how to stay composed through challenging situations, recover quickly, and perform while fatigued. All of these skills directly translate to the competitive shooting environment. Of all the training styles available, HIIT and hypertrophy stand out as my top recommendations. It builds the kind of athlete that thrives on the shooting line, especially when the pressure is on and there's no room for mental lapse. In this section, we'll explore HIIT workouts that challenge your limits and expand your potential.

Week 1-HIIT

Day 1 – AMRAP (As Many Rounds/Reps as Possible)

Workout: 20-minute AMRAP

- 250m row
- 10 push presses (dumbbells or barbell)
- 15 air squats
- 20 mountain climbers
- 30 seconds plank shoulder taps

About your workout:

Do the listed exercises in order, as many rounds as possible within 20 minutes. Pace yourself and focus on maintaining good form throughout. Your goal is to keep moving consistently for the entire time. Count how many full rounds you complete and write it down to track your progress.

Day 2 – For Time

Workout: 3 Rounds for Time

- 400m run
- 20 wall balls
- 15 burpees
- 10 dive bomber push-ups

About your workout:

Complete all 3 rounds of these exercises as quickly as you can, with good form. The clock runs until you're finished. Take rest when needed but push yourself to move with purpose. Record your finish time, you'll use it to measure progress in future workouts.

Day 3 – Completion

Workout: 3 Rounds, Complete at Your Pace

- 50m farmers carry
- 10 goblet squats
- 10 shoulder taps
- 15 burpees
- 30 seconds side plank (each side)

About your workout:

This workout is not timed. Focus on form, balance, and quality of movement. Move through each round deliberately. Use a weight that challenges you but still allows you to complete each exercise safely and with control.

Day 4 – Long Cardio + Grind

Workout: Every 4 minutes x 6 rounds (24 minutes total)

- 200m run or row
- 10 box jumps
- 12 Russian twists

About your workout:

Start a new round every 4 minutes. If you finish the round early, you get to rest for the remaining time. If a round takes you 3 minutes, you'll have 1 minute of rest before the next one begins. Stay consistent across all 6 rounds. Focus on quality reps and managing your energy.

Week 2-HIIT

Day 1 – AMRAP

Workout: 24-minute AMRAP

- 400m run
- 15 kettlebell swings
- 12 push-ups
- 10 jump squats
- 30 second plank

About your workout:

Repeat the full list of exercises as many times as you can in 24 minutes. Choose a moderate pace you can maintain. Take short breaks when needed, but keep moving and track how many rounds you finish.

Day 2 – For Time

Workout: 4 Rounds for Time

- 500m row
- 15 push-ups
- 10 box jumps
- 20 air squats
- 25 sit-ups

About your workout:

Complete 4 full rounds as quickly as you can, while staying in control of your movements. This one will challenge your cardio and muscular endurance. Record your total time to see improvement over time.

Day 3 – Completion

Workout: 4 Rounds

- 1-minute wall sit
- 12 step-ups (weighted if possible)
- 15 glute bridges
- 20 band pull-aparts
- 60 second plank

About your workout:

Move through each round at a controlled pace. This workout is focused on building strength, core control, and endurance. Don't worry about speed, focus on doing each rep well.

Day 4 – Long Cardio + Grind

Workout: 30-minute EMOM (Every Minute on the Minute)

- 1st minute: 12 burpees
- 2nd minute: 200m row
- 3rd minute: 15 dive bomber push-ups
- (Repeat this 3-minute cycle 10 times total)

About your workout:

This workout rotates every minute. Set a timer and begin the listed exercise for that minute. Once you finish it, rest until the next minute begins. It's a steady grind, so pace yourself and use the short rests to recover.

Week 3-HIIT

Day 1 – AMRAP

Workout: 20-minute AMRAP

- 500m row
- 10 box jumps
- 15 bent-over rows (dumbbells or barbell)
- 12 walking lunges
- 30 seconds wall sit

About your workout:

Do as many rounds as you can in 20 minutes. Don't rush, focus on steady breathing and proper form. This is a full-body challenge, especially for legs and back.

Day 2 – For Time

Workout: 21-15-9 reps for time

- Dumbbell snatches
- Goblet squats
- Sit-ups

About your workout:

Complete 21 reps of each exercise, then 15, then 9. Go fast, but stay in control. This workout is short and intense, so give it your best effort. Time yourself and write it down.

Day 3 – Completion

Workout: 3 Rounds

- 20m bear crawl
- 10 push-ups
- 15 kettlebell rows
- 10 lunges
- 1-minute plank

About your workout:

Complete 3 rounds at your own pace. Focus on quality over speed. This workout emphasizes body control, upper body strength, and core stability.

Day 4 – Long Cardio + Grind

Workout: Every 5 minutes x 5 rounds (25 minutes total)

- 400m run
- 15 dumbbell thrusters
- 10 sit-ups

About your workout:

Start a round every 5 minutes. If you finish the exercises in 3 minutes, you get 2 minutes rest. Use the rest time wisely, recover, hydrate, and get ready for the next round.

Week 4-HIIT

Day 1 – AMRAP

Workout: 22-minute AMRAP

- 400m run
- 12 pull-ups (assisted if needed) or TRX rows
- 10 push-ups
- 15 kettlebell deadlifts
- 20 flutter kicks

About your workout:

Cycle through this list for 22 minutes, doing as many rounds as possible. Modify pull-ups with TRX or band assistance if needed. Stay consistent and write down your total rounds.

Day 2 – For Time

Workout: 3 Rounds for Time

- 600m run
- 20 kettlebell swings
- 15 push presses
- 20 med ball sit-ups

About your workout:

Go through all 3 rounds as fast as you can. Longer runs make this a cardio challenge, so pace yourself early and push toward the end. Record your total time.

Day 3 – Completion

Workout: 4 Rounds

- 10 weighted lunges
- 30 second plank
- 15 bent-over rows (dumbbells or barbell)
- 1-minute air squat hold

About your workout:

Take your time on this one. It's about strength, stability, and endurance. Keep your form sharp and focus on breathing, especially during the isometric holds.

Day 4 – Long Cardio + Grind

Workout: 24-minute AMRAP

- 300m row
- 12 push-ups
- 15 kettlebell swings
- 20 step-ups

About your workout:

Work through this cycle as many times as you can in 24 minutes. Keep your pace steady and controlled. This workout blends cardio and functional strength, perfect for building stamina.

Week 5-HIIT

Day 1 – AMRAP

Workout: 25-minute AMRAP

- 250m row
- 20 med ball slams
- 12 dumbbell thrusters
- 30 walking lunges
- 1-minute plank

About your workout:

Push yourself to complete as many rounds as possible in 25 minutes. Stay consistent and pace your breathing. This is a high-output workout, so rest briefly when needed and keep moving.

Day 2 – For Time

Workout: 4 Rounds for Time

- 250m row
- 15 goblet squats
- 10 burpees
- 20 alternating lunges

About your workout:

Complete 4 rounds as quickly as you can. The row is your reset between sets. Push hard on the burpees and stay strong through the lunges. Record your time when finished.

Day 3 – Completion

Workout: 3 Rounds

- 20m walking lunges
- 15 scapular push-ups
- 30 seconds single-leg glute bridge (each leg)
- 15 bird dogs

About your workout:

Move with control and stability. This session strengthens stabilizers and improves posture. No timer, just focus on high-quality movement and activation.

Day 4 – Long Cardio + Grind

Workout: 20-minute Grind

Complete 5 Rounds of:

- 250m row
- 10 goblet squats
- 10 burpees

About your workout:

This is a straight grind, work through 5 rounds as efficiently as you can in 20 minutes. The combination of rowing and burpees will raise your heart rate, so use the squats to breathe and reset.

Week 6-HIIT

Day 1 – AMRAP

Workout: 26-minute AMRAP

- 400m run
- 10 burpees
- 20 Russian twists
- 15 sumo deadlift high pulls
- 50m farmers carry

About your workout:

Repeat this circuit for 26 minutes. It's a mix of cardio, core, and strength. Choose a moderate weight for the farmer's carry and sumo pulls. Maintain a steady effort throughout.

Day 2 – For Time

Workout: 5 Rounds for Time

- 400m run
- 10 box jumps
- 20 wall balls
- 15 V-ups

About your workout:

Complete all 5 rounds as quickly as you can. Stay sharp on the box overs and maintain good wall ball technique. Time yourself and push hard on the final round.

Day 3 – Completion

Workout: 4 Rounds

- 45 seconds row sprint
- 10 med ball cleans
- 12 wall sit dumbbell curls
- 15 side plank crunches

About your workout:

This workout targets strength and core under fatigue. Complete each movement with focus and control. Rest between rounds as needed. It's not timed, quality is the goal.

Day 4 – Long Cardio + Grind

Workout: 30-minute Mental Toughness Run

Every 4 minutes:

- Stop and do 10 burpees + 10 air squats

About your workout:

Run at a steady pace for 30 minutes. Every 4 minutes, stop and complete the bodyweight exercises, then continue running. This tests not only your physical endurance but your mental focus and discipline. Stick with it!

CHAPTER 10

THE BRIDGE BETWEEN BODY AND MIND

A Foundation Built on Movement

By now, you've probably realized this book isn't just about running plans or getting jacked. It's about something deeper. We've spent time digging into the physical side of archery: warm-ups, cardiovascular conditioning, muscular endurance, hypertrophy, and high-intensity interval training. But every step of the way, there's been a subtle thread connecting it all, which leads us somewhere beyond muscle, to the mind.

This chapter is the bridge.

We're going to tie everything together, including how movement shapes mental performance, how workouts sharpen focus and emotional control, and how your training plan is actually a blueprint for mental performance. Because if there's one lesson to carry forward, it's this:

Training your body is the first step in training your mind.

The Hidden Gains of Movement

You've felt it after a workout: clarity, calm, and confidence. That's not just feeling good; it's neuroscience.

When you move your body, especially through intentional physical training, you unlock powerful changes in the brain. Each workout becomes a cocktail of neurochemical benefits:

- BDNF (Brain-Derived Neurotrophic Factor): Fertilizes your brain's ability to grow, adapt, and learn new skills faster.
- Dopamine: Fuels motivation, goal-setting, and that addicting sense of progress.
- Serotonin: Stabilizes mood and helps you regulate emotions.
- Norepinephrine: Keeps you alert, focused, and ready to perform.
- Endorphins: Your natural painkillers and stress relievers.

These chemicals don't just make you feel better, they make you better. They prime your brain in all the right ways to elevate not only your confidence, but to elevate your archery game.

So every time you follow your training program, you're not just improving your physical ability. You're flooding your mind with tools to elevate your mental game. You're literally building the mind required to perform like a champion.

From Strength to Stillness: How Muscle Supports the Mind

Archery demands control, but that control isn't just about calming your nerves. It's about commanding your body. When you train for strength and stability, you build the physical trust that allows your mind to stop worrying and just execute.

When you train for stamina, you do more than shoot longer, you think better longer. Mental fatigue is the enemy of consistency, and it creeps in the moment your body starts to fatigue. The stronger your foundation, the less mental energy you waste just trying to hold yourself together. That energy becomes available for focus, adjustments, and flow.

You don't have to overthink every detail when your form holds up and your shot process feels easy and automatic. That's part of the point: to free your brain from managing the body so it can focus on executing the shot.

Fitness Is a Mental Skills Accelerator

Want to learn faster? Recover from mistakes quicker? Build the mindset of a pro?

Then move your body and exert yourself physically.

Every chapter in Part 1 demonstrates how physical training enhances skill development. When your body moves well, your brain learns faster. It's how human biology is wired. Movement is the natural trigger for brain change. That's why fit archers learn faster. That's why they retain skills longer. That's why they reset faster after a bad shot.

And that's why your physical routine is the first and best form of mental training.

Endurance of Body and Mind

In competition, the biggest challenges often show up late in the game, the last ends of a long day. That's when your heart is pounding, your arms are tired, and your brain starts whispering things you don't want to hear.

This is where training gets real.

Your muscles may burn, but so does your patience. Your legs may ache, but so does your confidence. Physical fatigue and mental fatigue show up together. That's why your training has to challenge both.

When you train under pressure or fatigue, doing SPTs, AMRAP sets, circuit training, or long runs, you're not just teaching your body to endure. You're teaching your mind to stay calm when it wants to quit. You're practicing presence when chaos creeps in. You're rehearsing the very mental state you'll need when the match is on the line.

You're inoculating yourself against breakdown.

This is how physical training becomes pressure training. It builds the callus your mind needs to thrive when it matters most.

Movement Rewires the Mind

Neuroplasticity isn't a buzzword; it's your brain's secret weapon and it's built through movement.

In Part 1, we explored how exercise enhances learning through:

- Creating new neurons
- Strengthening motor programs
- Improving focus and cognitive flexibility
- Increasing the brain's receptivity during "afterglow" windows

This isn't trivial information; it's critical. You are literally growing the brain you shoot with. This means your warm-ups, strength training, endurance circuits, and even post-practice walks aren't just add-ons. They are an engine to drive your improvement. They give your brain the raw material to wire new skills, rewire mental habits, and reinforce elite-level focus.

The Physical Path to Mental Mastery

Everything we do with our bodies, from the warm-up to the last rep, affects how we think, focus, recover, and perform under pressure. Archers who understand this connection elevate their entire process. They don't just shoot better. They think better. They recover faster. They show up stronger.

This is the new standard.

Where We Go Next: The Mental Game

You've laid the groundwork. You've trained your body to stabilize your shot and push through fatigue. More importantly, you've begun the real work of shaping the mind by shaping the body.

Now, we'll discuss the mental game.

In Part 2, we'll explore the tools of the mental game. These aren't mysterious superpowers. They're skills that are learnable, trainable, and repeatable.

Just like everything else in this book, they work for you, if you work them.

PART II

The Mental Game

CHAPTER 11

TRAINING THE MIND

The last chapters explored how physical training directly influences an archer's mindset, specifically, how exercise enhances focus, fitness builds emotional control, and strength supports confidence. But physical readiness is only half of the high-performance equation. Once your body is conditioned and consistent, your mind has to carry you through the pressure, plateaus, and gold medal moments. This chapter begins Part 2, where we move beyond the mental benefits of exercise into focused strategies for building a stronger mental game.

This is where you move beyond the gym and into the space between your ears. This is where pressure is no longer an obstacle but a training partner. In the coming chapters, we'll cover mental skills and habits that elite archers rely on every day, but which are accessible to anyone willing to train with purpose.

The mental side of archery doesn't begin on the shooting line, it starts long before, in the ways you approach your day, recover from mistakes, and view challenges. Unlike physical training, which often produces clear, visible results like more weight lifted, longer distances run, mental training is more subtle. But its impact is profound. In this section of the book, we'll cover the key pillars of mental performance:

Visualization

The first skill we'll cover is visualization. This is the mental rehearsal of our shot process or an event. It is more than daydreaming about shooting well. Neuroscience has shown that vividly imagining a motor skill activates many of the same neural circuits involved in physical execution. That means mental reps can supplement physical ones. You'll learn how to construct vivid imagery, time your visualizations, and use this tool for performance enhancement and recovery.

Positive Affirmations

Next, we'll explore positive affirmations, short, intentional statements that reshape internal dialogue. Your internal voice plays a massive role in handling stress and self-doubt. With effective affirmations, you'll build a belief system that supports your growth. But this isn't about repeating shallow slogans. You'll learn how to create affirmations that are specific, realistic, and tied to your process and your goals.

Mindfulness

Then, we'll dive into mindfulness. Archery demands presence like few other sports. It's about the here and now, not the arrow you just shot or the one you haven't even nocked yet. Mindfulness teaches you to stay centered, aware, and calm. It helps you notice tension before it builds, reset focus after a distraction, and enjoy the act of shooting form. You'll learn mindfulness exercises tailored for archers, including breathing techniques, body scans, and object-focused meditation.

Grit

Of course, none of this matters if you don't keep showing up, over and over. That's where grit comes in. Grit is about passion and perseverance for long-term goals. It carries you through the grind of training. We'll explore the science behind grit, how it can be developed through doing hard things, and how the fitness work from earlier chapters helps you build the mental durability required to thrive in archery.

Pressure Practice

Lastly, we'll get into pressure training. Shooting well in practice is one thing. Performing under pressure is another. This chapter will teach you how to simulate high-stakes conditions in training so you don't just hope to perform under pressure, you prepare for it. You'll learn drills that replicate the physiological stress of competition and develop emotional tools for staying sharp when it counts.

Each of these chapters will build on the others. Together, they form a mental training system you can apply in parallel with your physical training. Just as you tracked your reps and sets, you'll now track your thoughts, routines, and emotional patterns. You'll begin to see patterns like what helps you lock in and focus, what distracts and throws you off, and how to return to your baseline no matter the setting or environment.

So as you move into the next chapter, know that everything you've trained physically has prepared you for this. It's time to train your mind with the same purpose and intention. The same way you become proficient in the technical shot process through intentional practice and repetition, the mental game requires the same discipline, deliberate practice, and repetition. If you implement these mental strategies into your training, coupled with exercise and shooting, you will reach new heights and perform better than you ever have before.

CHAPTER 12

VISUALIZATION

Visualization is one of the most powerful tools an archer can use to strengthen their mental game and improve performance. It is the practice of mentally rehearsing a specific skill or scenario and seeing it unfold clearly in your mind. In archery, this means visualizing the shot process as vividly as possible. This technique builds a mental blueprint for success and conditions the brain to perform under pressure.

Psychologist Dr. Richard Suinn, who worked closely with Olympic athletes, introduced the term visual motor behavior rehearsal to describe this method. His research, as well as that of others in sports psychology, has shown that visualizing an action activates many of the same neural pathways as physically performing it. In other words, your brain doesn't distinguish the difference between visualization and physically practicing it. When done with focus and consistency, visualization enhances technical execution, reduces errors, and builds confidence, all without firing a single arrow. In fact, visualization is often described as a rehearsal for the mind, a way to repeatedly practice your perfect shot without risking fatigue, form breakdown, or injury.

There are several mechanisms by which visualization improves performance. First, it strengthens the neural pathways involved in the skill itself, priming the brain and body to execute smoothly when it matters. Second, it boosts confidence. Seeing yourself succeed, even if only in your mind, helps reinforce the belief that you can succeed. Visualization also helps reduce errors by mentally rehearsing perfect form, reducing the likelihood of common mistakes. Ultimately, it prepares the mind for pressure by creating familiarity with high-stakes scenarios, which in turn lowers anxiety and improves composure.

A famous study at the University of Chicago by Dr. Biasiotto illustrated the power of visualization. Three groups were tested on free-throw shooting, and a baseline score was recorded. For the next 30 days, one group practiced physically shooting the basketball, another visualized shooting daily, and a third did neither. After 30 days, the group who physically practiced improved by 24%, while the group who only practiced through visualization improved by 23%, almost the same as those who physically practiced. This underscores the profound impact of the mind in shaping real-world performance. Similar results have been shown across various sports, including archery.

2024 Paralympic Gold Medalist Matt Stutzman

In archery, where repetition and practice on the range shooting high arrow counts are often seen as the ultimate preparation, Matt

Stutzman's journey to the top of the Paralympic podium in Paris defies this convention. Known worldwide as The Armless Archer, Matt has inspired athletes with his seemingly impossible ability to shoot a bow using only his feet.

In the final months before the Games, Matt made a bold decision. He stopped shooting, not because he wanted to, but because life's full of big responsibilities. His demanding schedule left him with little time to train shooting at the range, so he leaned into the one tool he still had at his disposal: visualization.

Matt turned to visualization, practicing not with his bow in hand, or in Matt's case, bow in foot, but with his eyes closed. Day after day, he rehearsed every detail in his mind, including the venue's layout, the crowd's buzz, the pressure of the moment, and the feel of the wind brushing past his face. He visualized each step of his shot process. He imagined success, and he imagined adversity. He trained his mind to stay calm and focused no matter what scenario played out on that stage.

And when it came time to shoot for real, the mental blueprint he had built held strong.

It was with that blueprint that Matt Stutzman shot his way to Paralympic glory. It was a stunning validation of the power of mental preparation through visualization.

Matt's story isn't just inspirational, it's instructional. Visualization isn't a backup plan; it's a real form of training, capable of producing real results. Whether you're sidelined by injury, overwhelmed by schedule, or just seeking that extra edge, what you do with your mind matters. Mental reps count.

So how long should your visualization sessions be? Research indicates that consistency and quality matter more than sheer time. The ideal length is 10 to 15 minutes per session, practiced daily or at least 3 to 5 times per week. Short, frequent sessions are more effective than infrequent, longer ones. Structured visualization provides the most benefit, focusing on specific skills, routines, or pressure scenarios. The mental rehearsal should be vivid, intentional, and rich in sensory details. You should see it, feel it, hear it, and even experience the emotions of success.

The Shot Movie

One practical approach is the Shot Movie. The concept of the Shot Movie is attributed to Olympic gold medalist and author of an incredible book called With Winning in Mind, Lanny Bassham. In Bassham's words, the Shot Movie is a vivid mental rehearsal of the perfect performance, experienced through the eyes of the athlete. It involves visualizing the entire process of a successful shot while engaging all the senses: sight, sound, feel, and emotion. By mentally replaying this "movie" over and over, the athlete conditions their mind to expect success and execute consistently under pressure.

A Visualization Script

Creating your visualization script is another powerful technique. This is a personalized description of your perfect shot in vivid, first-person language. You should write this out and read it regularly before bed, before practice, or during recovery days. This reinforces your internal rhythm and boosts mental confidence. Your script becomes your performance anchor, a mental metronome that connects your mind and body.

Tournament Prep Visualization

Visualization can also be structured around specific competitive scenarios. For example, before an important tournament, you can visualize the warm-up area, the sound of the announcer, the texture of the field under your feet, the timer counting down, the music, and the final arrow of a match. Preparing your mind for these pressure moments reduces the likelihood of a stress-induced meltdown. You've seen it before, and you've succeeded before, in your mind.

After physically demanding practices, visualization becomes a tool for reinforcing composure and grit. Imagine yourself making a perfect shot while your muscles tremble and your sight picture is buzzing. See the arrow hit the center, not despite your exhaustion but because of your grit. This is a form of visualization that builds not only technical consistency but mental toughness. It trains your mind to perform through adversity and tough conditions.

Visualization Journal

Journaling can amplify the effects of visualization. You gain insight into your mental patterns by reflecting on what you visualized, how clear it was, what emotions surfaced, and how your confidence shifted. Over time, these reflections create a roadmap and a toolkit for self-regulation. I encourage you to use visualization logs to track daily habits: how long you visualized, what skill you focused on, what cue words you used, and how mentally sharp you felt after. This transforms visualization from an abstract idea into a measurable, trainable part of your performance plan. I've included an example below, including weekly reflection questions to help guide you.

Visualization Reflection Journal

In a notebook, use the guide below to deepen your visualization practice and evaluate its impact on your performance. The layout below can help you track your sessions and experiences over time.

Daily Practice Log

Date	Duration (min)	Focused Skill	Cue Word Used	Visualization Rating (1-5)	Notes/Emotions Felt

Date: Write down the date to track your sessions over time

Duration (min): Record how many minutes were devoted to the session. As a reminder, it's most beneficial to aim for 10-15 minute sessions; however, as a beginner to visualization, it may be easier to start with shorter 5-minute sessions or try to complete two 5-minute sessions at different times through the day.

Focused Skill: Just as our physical practice sessions should be intentional, our visualization sessions should follow the same structure. Reinforce the technique or skill you're working on during your shooting sessions in your visualization practice.

Cue Word Used: What are you saying to yourself in practice to keep yourself present throughout the shot cycle? We should use these same cues during visualization.

Visualization Rating (1-5): Rate your session with one being the worst and five being the best session ever.

Notes/Emotions Felt: Record any observations or emotions felt during the session.

Below are some weekly reflection questions you can answer and track over time to supplement your visualization journaling.

Weekly Reflection Questions

1. What specific shot detail was easiest to visualize this week? Why?
2. Where did your mind tend to wander during your visualizations?
3. How did your emotional state change before and after your visualization sessions?
4. Did visualization influence your physical performance in practice or competition this week? How so?
5. What external conditions (location, time of day, pre-visualization routine) seemed to support your most effective mental imagery?
6. What element of your visualization script or shot process do you want to improve or revise next week?

Practicing visualization also improves motor learning and the economy of movement. When archers mentally rehearse correct movement patterns, they reduce variability and increase efficiency.

According to research by Guillot and Collet, structured visualization supports the consolidation of motor programs, making physical execution smoother and more consistent. In a sport where millimeters matter, this refinement is a competitive edge.

The process of visualization creates a mental loop of success. When you rehearse calm, deliberate execution, your brain stores that pattern. The next time you approach the line; your subconscious draws from this library of experience. Visualization becomes more than a preparation technique; it becomes your competitive identity.

It is worth noting that visualization is a skill that improves with time and attention. Beginners may struggle to hold a clear mental image or stay focused for more than a few minutes. That's normal. Just like any form of training, consistency builds capacity and over time, your mental imagery becomes more vivid, your focus more stable, and your confidence more deeply rooted.

Reflect regularly on the quality of your visualization. Ask yourself: What aspects of the shot came easily? Where did your mind drift? What helped focus your attention? These moments of awareness sharpen your skills and guide your future sessions.

In closing, visualization is not a substitute for physical training, but it is an indispensable companion. It accelerates learning, prepares you for pressure, and enhances the clarity with which you execute your craft. It allows you to train when you can't shoot, to build belief before results arrive, and to script your performance long before the first whistle.

The best archers don't just shoot; they see and experience their success before it happens.

They step to the line with a mind rehearsed, a process internalized, and a shot they've already made a hundred times in their imagination. That's the power of visualization. And it's available to every archer willing to close their eyes and believe in the image they create.

CHAPTER 13

POSITIVE AFFIRMATIONS

Our thoughts are already shaping performance before the arrow hits the target. Positive affirmations are among the most accessible yet underutilized tools for rewiring the internal dialogue that drives confidence, focus, self-talk, and composure under pressure.

Your subconscious mind sets the boundaries for what you believe is possible, both at the high and low ends of your performance. This is your comfort zone, and it quietly governs how you act and react, even without you realizing it. One of the best analogies for how this works comes from driving a car. Imagine you're on the highway, lost in the music blaring from your car's speakers, and you glance down to see you're going 90 miles an hour. Instinctively, you ease off the gas, not because of a conscious decision, but because that speed exceeds your internal comfort zone.

On the other hand, if you look down and see you're only going 40 miles an hour, you'll naturally speed up to get back into your comfortable range. Your subconscious constantly nudges you back to what feels normal, even when you're not paying attention. The exact same thing happens in archery. If you begin scoring and your first half is higher than usual, your mind may pull you back down to your average scoring zone. If you start poorly, it might push you to recover and score higher in the second half. This is why adjusting your mental comfort zone is so critical; without that shift, your mind will work against your performance instead of supporting it.

This is where positive affirmations come in. These short, intentional statements, such as "I enjoy and am comfortable shooting strong, smooth shots under pressure," are designed to update your subconscious expectations. By repeating affirmations regularly, especially when paired with visualization, you begin to reshape what your mind accepts as your new baseline. Over time, the unfamiliar becomes familiar. What once felt like a stretch becomes your new standard.

The Science Behind Positive Affirmations

Research in cognitive neuroscience shows that the brain responds to affirmations by activating the reward centers and reducing the effects of stress. According to a 2015 study published in Social Cognitive and Affective Neuroscience, practicing self-affirmation increases activity in the ventromedial prefrontal cortex, a region associated with self-related processing and emotional regulation. This suggests that affirmations do more than boost mood; they create measurable changes in how the brain interprets challenge and stress.

Psychologist Claude Steele's Self-Affirmation Theory proposes that affirmations protect an individual's sense of self-integrity by reminding them of their core values. This form of mental reinforcement can guard against doubt and distraction for athletes, especially those in precision-based sports like archery. When an archer experiences internal or external stress, whether from a missed shot, rising expectations, or competition nerves, affirmations can stabilize focus and redirect energy toward the present moment.

In sports psychology, affirmations are often used to reinforce key mental cues, disrupt spirals of negative self-talk, and sharpen attention. By embedding powerful statements into your daily routine, you create a steady internal rhythm that can silence doubt and fuel confidence when it matters most. Just as physical practice strengthens muscle memory, mental repetition strengthens confidence.

By consciously feeding the brain new self-directed beliefs through affirmations, you're not just thinking positively, you're actually training your brain to raise its performance comfort zone. This allows you to sustain higher performance levels without self-sabotage or the internal resistance that often creeps in when we try to outshoot our old identity. In essence, affirmations are like quiet mental reps, building a stronger, more capable version of yourself from the inside out.

How to Create Effective Affirmations

Positive affirmations are short, specific, present-tense statements you say to yourself, usually written down and repeated regularly to reshape your subconscious beliefs. In archery, these affirmations help reset your mental comfort zone. They're not magical spells. They're mental cues that guide your expectations, behaviors, and performance.

A simple affirmation might be:

- "I enjoy and am comfortable shooting 300 arrows a day."
- "I enjoy and am comfortable executing strong, smooth shots in pressure situations."
- "I enjoy and am comfortable seeing my sight pin float and still shooting strong."

The purpose isn't just "positive thinking." It's neural conditioning. Your subconscious mind has an internal thermostat, it's constantly working to keep you inside the performance range it's most familiar with. If you push beyond that range without shifting your mental limits, your performance may fall back down to your average. But if your self-belief shifts first, performance can rise to meet it and stay there.

Positive affirmations help nudge that thermostat upward. Repetition makes the unfamiliar familiar. Over time, what once felt like a stretch becomes your new normal. And when that happens, pressure feels lighter, expectations feel right, and confidence feels earned.

Practicing Affirmations: Make It a Habit

To gain the full benefit of affirmations, repetition and visibility are key. Think of affirmations as mental nutrition; they need to be consumed regularly to have a lasting effect. One powerful practice is to write your affirmations on note cards. Choose three to five that reflect your current goals or areas for improvement and place them where you'll see them often: on your bathroom mirror, your bow case lid, your locker, or even on the dashboard of your car.

Saying them out loud, especially before practice or competition, builds a deeper neurological connection. When paired with calm, rhythmic breathing, affirmations can lower heart rate and reduce the mental clutter that sabotages focus. Over time, your affirmations will become internalized, rising automatically during moments of doubt or intensity.

Update your affirmations regularly. As your mindset and goals evolve, your internal dialogue should too.

Affirmation Examples for Archers

Here are a few affirmations specifically tailored for archers:

- I enjoy and am comfortable trusting my shot process.
- I enjoy and am comfortable shooting under pressure.
- I enjoy and am comfortable with my sight's natural movement.
- I enjoy and am comfortable responding to challenges with poise.
- I enjoy and am comfortable shooting 300 arrows in training.

Each of these statements is short, vivid, and immediately actionable. They don't describe a result, they describe the mindset that leads to results.

Positive Affirmation Journal & Practice Sheet

Tracking your affirmation habits can help you build consistency and observe their impact on your mental state over time. Use the following table as a tool to reflect on how affirmations feel throughout the day:

Daily Affirmation Routine

Time of Day	Affirmation	Setting (e.g., mirror, range)	Emotional Response
Morning:			
Pre-Practice:			
Evening:			

In addition to logging your sessions, take time each week to reflect on them.

Weekly Reflection Questions

1. Which affirmation felt the most powerful this week? Why?
2. Did you notice changes in your mindset or behavior after using affirmations?
3. When during the day did affirmations feel most effective?
4. What negative thoughts did you replace using your affirmations?
5. What affirmations need to be revised, added to, or removed?

By answering these questions, you not only reinforce the habit of self-reflection but also refine your mental dialogue in a way that better serves you.

Affirmations are not magic; they're mental training reps. They don't guarantee a perfect score, but they do shape the mindset you bring to the line. With every repetition, you are affirming who you are becoming as an archer. You are quieting the noise, steadying your breath, and rooting your identity in belief. And over time, those words you once repeated to convince yourself become the truth you live on the shooting line. That's the lasting power of affirmations.

Reflection Questions

1. What are the dominant thoughts or beliefs I carry about myself as an archer? Are they helping me or holding me back?
2. Do I ever catch myself using negative self-talk before, during, or after a shot? What impact does that have on my performance?

3. If my subconscious is always listening, what message have I been feeding it lately?

4. What areas of my shooting do I feel the most insecure about, and how could I rewrite those beliefs as positive affirmations?

5. How comfortable am I with the idea of saying affirmations out loud or writing them down? If I feel resistance, where might that be coming from?

6. Can I think of a time when a change in mindset or belief helped me break through a plateau or perform better under pressure?

7. What would it look like if I truly believed in my ability to improve, succeed, and compete at the highest level? What affirmations would that version of me repeat every day?

8. How could I incorporate positive affirmations into my daily training routine? What time or trigger would help me make them a habit?

9. What is one limiting belief I want to let go of, and what new belief do I want to replace it with?

10. How would my performance change if I started expecting success instead of fearing failure? What affirmation captures that mindset shift?

CHAPTER 14

MINDFULNESS

Leading up to the Paralympic Games in Paris, I worked closely with the team to develop personalized cues. I would repeat these short, meaningful words or phrases from the coach's box during each arrow. Now, on the surface, this might seem unnecessary. After all, these athletes know their shot process inside and out. But the power of these verbal cues isn't in instruction, it's in attention. In an environment where 8,000 spectators are cheering, music is blaring, cameras are rolling, and pressure is unbelievably high, even the best archers can slip out of the present moment.

Each cue or phrase serves as an anchor. It pulls the archer out of the chaos and back into their shot process. Not the last one, not the outcome, not the noise, but the process happening right now. It's a simple practice, but a profound one. This is mindfulness in action. Using deliberate, present-tense language to bring focus and calm to the chaos. When the archer hears my cue, it's not just a reminder of what to do. It's a reminder of where the mind should be.

The slightest lapse in attention can be the difference between a ten and an eight in archery. Success is measured in millimeters, and the archer's ability to remain present in each moment is essential. Mindfulness is being consciously aware of your thoughts, sensations, and surroundings, and is one of the most effective tools an archer can train. This chapter explores mindfulness, why it matters for archery performance, and how to build it into your training routine in a structured and impactful way.

Mindfulness is a form of mental strength, an active awareness that grounds you in the present and calms internal noise. For the archer, this means developing the ability to focus on one arrow at a time, free from distractions, emotion, or thoughts of the future. Mindfulness trains the archer to respond rather than react, to observe without judgment, and to remain composed regardless of the outcome.

Scientific research supports the performance benefits of mindfulness. Studies have shown that mindfulness training enhances attentional control, reduces anxiety, and improves emotional regulation, all critical factors in competitive archery. One study found that consistent mindfulness practice leads to functional and structural changes in areas of the brain associated with attention, self-awareness, and emotional regulation. It is also reported that mindfulness-trained military personnel showed better working memory and fewer attentional lapses under stress. Athletes who regularly practice mindfulness demonstrate greater consistency under pressure, a more adaptive response to stress, and quicker recovery from mistakes. This mental clarity offers a competitive edge in a sport where the margin for error is minimal.

Mindfulness also complements the physical training covered earlier in this book, just as cardiovascular and strength training condition the body, mindfulness conditions the brain. It develops the mental muscles of awareness, stillness, and self-regulation. This cooperation between body and mind creates a holistic performance model, where mental steadiness amplifies physical precision. An archer who trains mindfulness is better equipped to execute under fatigue, maintain poise in shoot-offs, and recover after poor shots.

Building mindfulness into your archery practice doesn't require hours of meditation. It starts with simple, deliberate moments of focus. Begin by incorporating a mindful breathing practice before each session. Sit or stand quietly and take five deep breaths, noticing the rhythm of your inhale and exhale. Let this become a transition into your training, signaling your mind to arrive in the present. Focus entirely on what you are doing in the moment, not what you've done or what comes next. Over time, this consistent mindfulness rewires your brain for deeper concentration and steadier performance.

I like using a single Raisinette to strengthen present-moment awareness further, but any small chocolate candy can work. Place the candy in your hand and observe its shape, color, and texture. Slowly bring it to your nose and notice the smell. Place it in your mouth, but don't chew it. Let it sit on your tongue and take notice of the smoothness of the chocolate, the subtle texture as it melts, the changing sensation as it softens. Now bite into it and feel the transition in texture and taste. This exercise, though simple, trains your mind to fully experience a moment. Practicing this type of sensory immersion regularly builds the skill of present moment awareness that you can later apply to your shot process.

You can also practice mindfulness outside of archery. Incorporate short, daily mindfulness exercises such as walking or running without your phone, eating alone in a quiet place, or journaling your thoughts. These simple practices strengthen your mental presence in everyday life and make it more accessible on the shooting line. Athletes who cultivate mindfulness as a lifestyle, not just a training tool, report lower stress, improved sleep, and greater emotional stability.

An excellent way to train mindfulness in archery is through a routine called mindful shooting. Set aside a blank bale practice session, and commit to shooting ten arrows with complete attention to each shot cycle. No score, no judgment, just full awareness. After each arrow, pause, breathe, and assess your mental state. Were you present? Distracted? Calm? Over time, you'll become more attuned to your internal state and thoughts and better able to regulate them.

In the same way a coach uses cueing, you can also use mental cues or mantras on your own. You can repeat these short words or phrases before or during your shot process to pull yourself into the moment. Take some time to develop some of your own cues and implement them in your practice sessions to determine which ones are most effective for you. Over time, these cues become anchors that help you return to the present during high-pressure moments.

Mindfulness is not about becoming emotionless or immune to pressure. It's about becoming aware of those emotions and choosing how to respond. A mindful archer doesn't pretend the stakes don't matter; they refuse to let anxiety dictate their actions. This composure is a learned skill, one that grows with practice.

Reflection Questions

1. When I'm on the shooting line, where is my attention usually focused (the past, the future, or the present)? How does that affect my performance?
2. What specific thoughts or distractions tend to pull me out of the present moment during training or competition?
3. Have I ever had a moment in archery where I felt completely present, calm, and in control? What contributed to that feeling?
4. What cues or phrases could help anchor me to the present moment during high-pressure situations? How can I integrate those into my routine?
5. Do I have a consistent routine that promotes focus and presence before each shot? If not, what small step could I take to build one?
6. What simple daily habit (e.g., breathwork, journaling, cue building) could I practice to build mindfulness both on and off the range?

CHAPTER 15

GRIT

I witnessed the same story play out at two different tournaments in two different countries.

In the Czech Republic, Para Archer Timothy Palumbo was very sick the night before and into the morning of his qualification round. He was pale, dehydrated, and miserable. Back in the United States at Collegiate Target Nationals, Madison Abel, one of my collegiate archers at University of Rio Grande, was going through the same thing. She was sick, throwing up, and weak.

Neither of these athletes know each other. They weren't at the same event. But they were both met with the same conversation. "You can throw up between ends if you need to. That's fine. But I need you to stay strong and shoot through it." And they did.

Palumbo pulled himself together and pushed through every end of qualification. He didn't just finish; he shot his personal best qualification score. Madison, stomach still turning, competed in team rounds with the women's barebow team and played a part in them earning a national championship together.

That's what grit looks like. It's not glamorous. It doesn't feel good in the moment. But it's the choice to keep going when your body and brain are begging you to stop. It's showing up, fully committed, even when the circumstances are far from ideal.

Most people think grit is about being tough. But it's really about deciding in advance that your goals are worth more than how you feel. And in those moments, Tim and Madison showed exactly what that looks like in real life.

What Is Grit?

Grit is sticking with something you care about, even when it's hard, boring, or frustrating. It's showing up, day after day, through setbacks, slow progress, and challenging moments, and choosing not to quit, even when it would be easier to walk away. Psychologist Angela Duckworth, whose research brought this concept to the forefront, defines grit as a blend of two core traits: perseverance and passion for long-term goals. In her bestselling book Grit: The Power of Passion and Perseverance, she emphasizes that what often distinguishes top performers from their peers isn't raw talent; it's their ability to endure. To stick with difficult things. To care deeply and keep going when it's no longer fun or easy.

Duckworth's research in diverse populations from West Point cadets to spelling bee finalists and Olympic hopefuls consistently reveals that grit is one of the strongest predictors of long-term success. This certainly holds true in archery, which demands consistency over months and years.

In archery, grit looks like showing up on the days when you just don't feel like shooting. It's choosing another end of blank bale arrows instead of quitting early. Grit doesn't mean you love every moment of training; it means you're committed to it even when you don't.

Why Grit Matters in Archery

Archery rewards those who endure. Improvements are often incremental, barely visible day to day. Entire competitions can hinge on one arrow. Training cycles are long, and breakthroughs come after weeks, sometimes months, of what feels like stagnation. The athlete who stays consistent, learns from setbacks, and keeps working anyway inevitably passes the one who burns bright but fades fast.

Grit is also crucial for weathering the emotional highs and lows of competition. Every archer has faced slumps, setbacks, losses, and even their "worst day ever." Grit is the engine that pulls you forward, turning failure into feedback and disappointment into determination. Gritty archers don't just survive difficulty; they grow through it. They make peace with the monotony of the daily grind. They work on the boring things because they know mastery happens through perfecting basic fundamentals.

Grit Is Built, Not Born

One of the most empowering realities from Duckworth's research is that grit is malleable. It's not a fixed trait but a skill that can be cultivated with time, effort, and intention. People become grittier through experience, especially when they learn to frame difficulty as part of the process, not a sign they're doing something wrong.

Effort counts twice, Duckworth explains. Talent x effort = skill. Skill x effort = achievement. In other words, consistent effort compounds. It turns raw potential into usable ability and then turns ability into performance.

This is another connection to Part 1 of this book. Physical training, whether strength work, cardio, or endurance, builds both fitness and fortitude. Every time you finish a hard workout when you're sore, or stick to your run schedule in the rain, you're laying down neural and psychological patterns of persistence. The discipline to train your body becomes the same discipline that helps you hold focus through a difficult match or rebuild after a rough end. It's grit.

How Physical Fitness Strengthens Grit

Through the earlier chapters of this book, you've already encountered demanding workouts from hypertrophy, long runs, and high-intensity circuits. These weren't just about shaping your body; they were about shaping your mind. Physical routines, especially when adhered to over weeks and months, mirror the same qualities that define grit: showing up consistently, pushing through fatigue, and tolerating discomfort without quitting.

Studies support this. One found that people who engage in consistent, goal-oriented physical training score higher on grit scales and report greater emotional resilience. It's no coincidence that elite military training, Olympic pipelines, and high-level sports all emphasize physical challenge; it's a vessel for mental toughness.

When you do hard things by choice, you prepare your nervous system and your identity to endure them under pressure.

Archery-Specific Applications: Grit in Action

Let's take a closer look at what grit looks like on the range:

- An archer training outdoors, not skipping sessions when it's cold, raining, or both.
- A collegiate athlete rebuilding their shot after a major form breakdown, trusting the long game over quick fixes.
- A Paralympic hopeful completing their daily strength work even during rehab or fatigue.

These athletes don't succeed in spite of challenges, they succeed because they've trained through them.

Doing hard things becomes a habit. A mental callus. A part of your identity. You become the kind of athlete who doesn't fold under pressure.

Practical Grit-Building Strategy: The 4-Week Challenge

To make grit tangible, try this training experiment. For four weeks, commit to one physical challenge and one archery challenge. Show up daily, even when you don't want to. Track it with a simple "Did the work." This builds an identity loop. Each day you show up, you reinforce: "I'm someone who finishes what I start."

A full tracker and reflection prompts are included later in this chapter. Use it!

Growth Mindset + Grit = Long-Term Mastery

Grit grows best in athletes who also believe they can improve. That's the foundation of a growth mindset. Carol Dweck's research showed that when athletes believe their abilities are developable, not fixed, they respond to failure with effort, not avoidance.

Pairing a growth mindset with grit creates a powerful feedback loop. You don't fear setbacks. You use them. You believe effort works, so you're more likely to give it. You see progress as nonlinear, so you don't panic when it stalls. You're not just resilient. You're relentless.

The Archer Who Keeps Showing Up

Competitive archery favors those who outlast. Your form may evolve, and equipment may change. But if you can keep working, day after day, season after season, you'll build a kind of strength that even goes beyond the shooting line. That's what grit delivers: not perfection, but perseverance. Not immunity from setbacks, but a fierce response to them.

Train your body. Challenge your limits. Stick to your routines even when they lose their novelty. And when it gets hard, don't flinch. You're not here for easy. You're here for excellence.

4-Week Grit Challenge Tracker

Instructions:

Each day, complete one physical challenge and one archery challenge—these can be customized based on your training goals (examples below). Mark completion with ☑ and log a brief note about how it felt. Once per week, complete the reflection prompts.

Customize Your Challenges:

Physical Challenge Ideas:

- – 20-minute run or walk
- – 100 push-ups/sit-ups split throughout the day
- – Yoga or stretching session
- – Complete your strength training workout

Archery Challenge Ideas:

- – Shoot 30–60 arrows (indoor/outdoor)
- – 10-minute blank bale + journaling
- – Daily mental reps/visualization practice
- – Practice pre-shot routine 5x with perfect form

WEEK 1

Day	Physical Challenge	Archery Challenge	Did a "Hard Thing"?	Reflection Word/Phrase
Mon.	☐	☐	☐	
Tues.	☐	☐	☐	
Wed.	☐	☐	☐	
Thu.	☐	☐	☐	
Fri.	☐	☐	☐	
Sat.	☐	☐	☐	
Sun.	☐	☐	☐	

Weekly Reflection:

- What challenged me the most this week?
- What am I most proud of?
- How did I respond on the days I didn't feel like doing it?

WEEK 2

Day	Physical Challenge	Archery Challenge	Did a "Hard Thing"?	Reflection Word/Phrase
Mon.	☐	☐	☐	
Tues.	☐	☐	☐	
Wed.	☐	☐	☐	
Thu.	☐	☐	☐	
Fri.	☐	☐	☐	
Sat.	☐	☐	☐	
Sun.	☐	☐	☐	

Weekly Reflection:

- Did I get mentally stronger this week? How?
- What patterns am I noticing about my motivation?
- What mindset helped me finish even when it was tough?

WEEK 3

Day	Physical Challenge	Archery Challenge	Did a "Hard Thing"?	Reflection Word/Phrase
Mon.	☐	☐	☐	
Tues.	☐	☐	☐	
Wed.	☐	☐	☐	
Thu.	☐	☐	☐	
Fri.	☐	☐	☐	
Sat.	☐	☐	☐	
Sun.	☐	☐	☐	

Weekly Reflection:

- What "hard thing" made me grow this week?
- How do I feel about consistency now vs. before?
- What distractions did I overcome?

WEEK 4

Day	Physical Challenge	Archery Challenge	Did a "Hard Thing"?	Reflection Word/Phrase
Mon.	☐	☐	☐	
Tues.	☐	☐	☐	
Wed.	☐	☐	☐	
Thu.	☐	☐	☐	
Fri.	☐	☐	☐	
Sat.	☐	☐	☐	
Sun.	☐	☐	☐	

Weekly Reflection:

- What have I learned about my limits—and my grit?
- How will I carry this grit into competition season?
- What identity am I building with these habits?

Grit Statement (After Week 4)

Write one sentence that captures your growth through this challenge:

"I am the kind of archer who

_____."

Reflection Questions

1. When was the last time I felt like giving up on something important to me? What did I do in that moment, and why?

2. Do I tend to push through tough situations, or do I find myself backing off when things get challenging? Why do I respond that way?

3. What long-term goal am I currently working toward? How do I stay motivated when progress feels slow or invisible?

4. How do I respond to setbacks, failure, or plateaus? Do I view them as reasons to stop or chances to grow?

5. Who in my life demonstrates grit in a way I admire? What can I learn from them?

6. What habits or routines help build my resilience on tough days? How can I make those part of my training process?

7. Is my commitment to my goals stronger than my desire for comfort or convenience? If not, what needs to change?

8. What is one thing I can commit to doing this week that will strengthen my mental toughness and grit?

CHAPTER 16

PRESSURE PRACTICE

Accomplishing something great isn't supposed to be easy. By definition, it demands more. It takes us beyond what's comfortable, past our normal limits. And when we take on something meaningful, pressure shows up. Pressure from time constraints. Pressure from peers. Pressure from people counting on us. Pressure from expectations, whether our own or others'.

But here's the truth: achieving something great without pressure is nearly impossible. If someone says, "Take as long as you want, there are no obstacles, and if you fail, no one will care," how will that pursuit shape you? There's no risk. No weight. No transformation. Anyone can walk that path.

Pressure, on the other hand, sharpens people. It brings out both the best and the worst. It's the fire where potential melts or is forged into something stronger. I've seen athletes grow right in front of my eyes just from performing under pressure. It changes how they see themselves; they walk taller, feel tougher, and believe nothing can beat them.

You Have to Create Pressure to Learn to Handle It

As a coach, you owe it to your athletes to give them real experiences with pressure, not to break them, but to build them. They have to feel it. They have to handle it. They have to overcome it. Otherwise, how can you expect them to do it when it matters most?

Intentionally create situations in practice where the odds are stacked against them. Set up drills where the possibility of success is slim. A goal that requires perfection under pressure, like 10 perfect shots in a row, where each team member shoots one arrow at a time. If anyone misses a 10, the count starts over. By the way, they don't stop until the challenge is completed or gets too dark to shoot. This is a telling drill we utilize at the University of Rio Grande. You begin to see the patterns: some players never miss, even as the 8th, 9th, or 10th shooter in the lineup. Others crack every time. You can learn a lot from these observations.

You have to test for this. You can't wait until the event to find out who can handle the pressure. It needs to be part of your daily training, a natural part of how you build awareness and toughness, and help others improve.

You Don't Rise to the Occasion, You Sink to the Level of Your Training

When the moment comes, the big tournament, the gold medal match, the single arrow shootoff, you don't magically rise to some superhero version of yourself. You drop to your default, which is whatever you've practiced. If you and your team train at a mediocre level, don't be surprised when you underperform in high-stakes moments. If your team practices at an elite level, even under pressure, then your "drop" is still better than most people's peak. That's why every practice has to count. Every rep needs to build the foundation that will hold up under pressure. Pressure is not just a moment. It's a skill. And like any skill, it must be trained.

The best archers don't just train technique. They train mind, body, and they test these things under pressure by simulating stress. They expose themselves to environments that mimic pressure so that when the real moment comes, it feels familiar. They don't hope they'll hold it together; they know they can because they've practiced it.

The Problem With Comfortable Practice

Practice is safe and quiet. There's no scoreboard, no medal, and for the most part, no one's watching. In that setting, it's easy to feel in control. But performance in competition doesn't come from what you can do in practice. It comes from what you can do under stress. And, as you likely know, stress changes things.

When your heart rate rises, when you're shaking, and when thoughts speed up, your access to the fine motor control and mental clarity you rely on in practice can fade. That's why archers who shoot amazing practice rounds often feel confused when they fall apart under pressure. It's not necessarily a flaw; it's a lack of exposure. If you never train under pressure, your brain doesn't know how to handle it.

Training the Response, Not Avoiding the Feeling

You'll never remove pressure from competition. But you can train how you respond to it.

High-level athletes understand that pressure isn't the enemy, uncontrolled reactions are. Research in performance psychology shows that how you interpret physiological symptoms of pressure influence your outcome. In a 2014 study published in the Journal of Experimental Psychology, athletes who viewed nerves as helpful rather than harmful performed significantly better under stress. Mindset matters and it's something you can develop through training.

The goal of pressure training is not to simulate discomfort for the sake of toughness. It's to expand your comfort zone so that challenge feels manageable and even expected.

Pressure Practice Strategies for Archers

Below are several ways to integrate pressure into your training intentionally and constructively:

1. Shoot and Score in Front of Others

Have a coach, teammate, or even a friend watch and record your score as you shoot. The simple act of being observed raises your stress level. Set a goal and let someone else hold you to it.

2. Consequence Rounds

Set stakes for your performance. If you don't shoot a set number of 10s or reach a certain score, there's a consequence. It could be 100 pushups, running laps, or shooting extra arrows. The key here is accountability. Pressure without consequences isn't pressure at all.

3. Replicate the Match Format

Train in the format you compete in, end length, arrow count, timing, and match structure. Set up your timer. Stand next to someone. Move between lines. Practice tiebreakers and shoot-offs. Make tournament day feel like just another practice day.

4. Compete in Practice

Mini-tournaments in training can give athletes the repetition of shooting head-to-head. Track wins, play elimination games, utilize brackets. Even if the prizes are small or silly, the stakes feel very real.

5. Distraction

Create scenarios with loud music, crowd noise, or even teammates shouting or mock commentary. These chaotic drills help condition your ability to focus on what matters: your process.

6. Pressure Cue Integration

Pair your mental cues or affirmations with high-stress shooting. Teach your brain to associate phrases like "here I go" or "strong and smooth" with staying grounded in pressure. It anchors your attention and reduces feelings of panic.

Pressure in Real Life

I've seen pressure training pay off in unforgettable ways. I've coached archers who didn't just survive through high-pressure situations, they thrived in them. Why? Because they trained for it.

If you didn't catch Matt Stutzman's incredible run at the Paralympic Games, from his early matches all the way through his gold medal final, it's worth going back to watch. Rather than letting the intensity of the moment, the noise, or the crowd distract his focus, Matt took control of his emotions and used the energy of the arena to his advantage. He didn't shy away from the spotlight; he embraced it, even played to the crowd like the showman he is.

Pressure isn't something to avoid. It's something to train for, adapt to, and ultimately use to your advantage, just like Matt did.

Are You Ready for the Real Thing?

Ask yourself:

- How often do I intentionally train under conditions that mimic pressure?
- When I feel nerves, how do I respond? Do I have a plan or just hope it goes away?
- What mental cue or phrase helps me return to focus under stress?
- What small step can I take this week to stretch my comfort zone?

Make Pressure Your Training Partner

Pressure isn't the enemy of performance; it's the proving ground. The more you expose yourself to it in training, the more you teach your mind and body how to manage it, or even leverage it.

Eventually, the arrow to decide the outcome of a match, the noisy crowd, the medal on the line, it all feels familiar. Not because it's easy, but because you've trained for it.

That's what makes champions: not just great shooters, but great performers, especially when it counts.

CHAPTER 17

THE PATH FORWARD

This is where the book ends.

You now hold more than information. You hold a blueprint. A complete system designed to develop not just your body, not just your mind, but the impactful relationship between the two. And with that system, you have the power to transform your performance.

You've read about how exercise sharpens focus, calms the nervous system, and builds mental toughness. You've trained your mind through the power of visualization, affirmations, pressure training, and mindfulness. You've explored how strength training and conditioning do more than build muscle.

But reading is not enough.

From Reading to Action

Now it's your turn.

You've learned the tools, the systems, the drills, and the science. But mastery doesn't come from knowing. It comes from doing.

Here's how to begin:

1. Choose one training path from Part 1. Stick with it for 4–6 weeks. Track your workouts and your progress.
2. Practice one or two mental skills from Part 2 every day. Consistent practice adds up. Commit to the process of training these mental skills.
3. Shape and build your identity through positive affirmations and intentional reflection.
4. Use pressure as a teacher. Don't avoid it, train for it.

This is not the end. It's the start of your next chapter.

Now go write it.

REFERENCES

Cotman, C. W., & Berchtold, N. C. (2002). Exercise: A behavioral intervention to enhance brain health and plasticity. *Trends in Neurosciences*, 25(6), 295–301.

Erickson, K. I., et al. (2011). Exercise training increases size of hippocampus and improves memory. *PNAS*, 108(7), 3017–3022.

Voss, M. W., et al. (2013). Bridging animal and human models of exercise-induced brain plasticity. *Trends in Cognitive Sciences*, 17(10), 525–544.

Ratey, J. J. (2008). *Spark: The revolutionary new science of exercise and the brain*. Little, Brown Spark.

Winter, B., et al. (2007). High impact running improves learning. *Neurobiology of Learning and Memory*, 87(4), 597–609.

Behm, D. G., & Chaouachi, A. (2011). A review of the acute effects of static and dynamic stretching on performance. *European Journal of Applied Physiology*, 111(11), 2633–2651.

Hillman, C. H., Erickson, K. I., & Kramer, A. F. (2008). Be smart, exercise your heart: Exercise effects on brain and cognition. *Nature Reviews Neuroscience*, 9(1), 58–65.

Tomporowski, P. D., et al. (2008). Exercise and children's intelligence, cognition, and academic achievement. *Educational Psychology Review*, 20, 111–131.

Duckworth, A. (2016). *Grit: The power of passion and perseverance*. Scribner.

Maddi, S. R., et al. (2006). Hardiness and performance in elite military training. *Consulting Psychology Journal: Practice and Research*, 58(3), 187–200.

Dweck, C. S. (2006). *Mindset: The new psychology of success*. Random House.

Schoenfeld, B. J. (2010). The mechanisms of muscle hypertrophy and their application to resistance training. *Journal of Strength and Conditioning Research*, 24(10), 2857–2872.

American College of Sports Medicine. (2018). *ACSM's Guidelines for Exercise Testing and Prescription* (10th ed.). Lippincott Williams & Wilkins.

Kraemer, W. J., & Ratamess, N. A. (2004). Fundamentals of resistance training: Progression and exercise prescription. *Medicine & Science in Sports & Exercise*, 36(4), 674–688.

Hillman, C. H., et al. (2009). The effect of acute treadmill walking on cognitive control and academic achievement in preadolescent children. *Neuroscience*, 159(3), 1044–1054.

Meeusen, R., et al. (2013). Brain neurotransmitters in fatigue and overtraining. *Applied Physiology, Nutrition, and Metabolism*, 38(5), 657–664.

Suinn, R. M. (1984). Visual motor behavior rehearsal for athletes. *The Behavior Therapist*, 7, 124–126.

Biasiotto, M. (1996). Mental practice and free-throw shooting accuracy. *University of Chicago Study* [Unpublished report].

Bassham, L. R. (2011). *With winning in mind: The mental management system: An Olympic champion's success system* (3rd ed.). Mental Management Systems.

Guillot, A., & Collet, C. (2008). Construction of the motor imagery integrative model in sport: A review and theoretical investigation. *International Review of Sport and Exercise Psychology*, 1(1), 31–44.

Cascio, C. N., O'Donnell, M. B., Tinney, F. J., Lieberman, M. D., Taylor, S. E., Strecher, V. J., & Falk, E. B. (2016). Self-affirmation activates brain systems associated with self-related processing and reward and is reinforced by future orientation. *Social Cognitive and Affective Neuroscience, 11(4)*, 621–629.

Steele, C. M. (1988). The psychology of self-affirmation: Sustaining the integrity of the self. In L. Berkowitz (Ed.), Advances in experimental social psychology (Vol. 21, pp. 261–302). Academic Press.

Gotink, R. A., Meijboom, R., Vernooij, M. W., Smits, M., & Hunink, M. G. (2016). 8-week mindfulness based stress reduction induces brain changes similar to traditional long-term meditation practice: A systematic review. *Brain and Cognition, 108*, 32–49.

Calderone, A. (2024). Neurobiological changes induced by mindfulness and MBSR: Enhancing emotional regulation and anxiety reduction. *Frontiers in Neuroscience*.

Kabat-Zinn, J. (1990). *Full catastrophe living: Using the wisdom of your body and mind to face stress, pain, and illness*. Delacorte.

Jha, A. P., et al. (2007). Examining the protective effects of mindfulness training on working memory capacity and affective experience. *Emotion*, 10(1), 54–64.

Jha, A. P., Morrison, A. B., Parker, S. C., & Stanley, E. A. (2015). Minds "at attention": Mindfulness training curbs attentional lapses in military cohorts. *PLOS ONE, 10*(2), e0116889.

Tang, Y. Y., et al. (2015). The neuroscience of mindfulness meditation. *Nature Reviews Neuroscience*, 16(4), 213–225.

Mustaza, M. S. A., & Kutty, F. (2022). The relationship between grit personality and resilience. *Creative Education, 13(10),* 3255–3269.

Brooks, A. W. (2014). Get excited: Reappraising pre-performance anxiety as excitement improves performance. Journal of Experimental Psychology: General, 143(3), 1144–1158.

ABOUT THE AUTHOR

Jonathan Clemins is the Head Coach of the USA Paralympic Archery Team and a seasoned coach at the collegiate and elite levels. With years of experience guiding athletes to national titles, world championships, and Paralympic glory, Clemins combines a deep understanding of sports science with a passion for developing confident, high-performing archers.

He trains athletes in a way that honors how human beings are designed, physiologically, socially, and psychologically, creating a holistic system that helps athletes fire on all cylinders and perform at their absolute best.